THE MINISTER AS MORAL COUNSELOR

Gaylord Noyce

ABINGDON PRESS
NASHVILLE

THE MINISTER AS MORAL COUNSELOR

Copyright © 1989 by Abingdon Press

This book is printed on acid-free paper.

Library of Congress Cataloging-in-Publication Data

Noyce, Gaylord B.
   The minister as moral counselor / Gaylord Noyce.
     p. cm.
  Bibliography: p.
  ISBN 0-687-26961-X (pbk.: alk. paper)
  1. Pastoral counseling. 2. Christian ethics. I. Title.
BV4012.2.N69   1989
253.5—dc19   88-39300
                                                           CIP

MANUFACTURED BY THE PARTHENON PRESS AT
NASHVILLE, TENNESSEE, UNITED STATES OF AMERICA

*To those many students
who have shared their own wisdom and faith with me
in our mutual learning of ministry.*

Foreword

A NUMBER OF THREADS HAVE WOVEN THEM-
selves into my experience to provoke this book. One of these
threads has been the problematic relationship of pastoral
care and moral concern in the church. Often, when pastors
have tried to be faithful to their best insights for the one,
they have wondered whether they were betraying the other.
The pastoral counseling movement owes an enormous debt
to psychology and psychotherapeutic practice. As a result,
the ordained minister's "nondirective," parishioner-cen-
tered pastoral care has seemed to require playing down the
"prophetic" dimension of ministry and the task of moral
guidance. And the unavoidable moral claims of Scripture
and tradition prompt preaching and teaching that seem to
go against interpersonal rapport and empathy.

Another thread has been my experience in teaching
seminarians. Students and I have repeatedly struggled with
the problem of vocational identity in light of all the
variegated expectations laid on anyone occupying the
pastoral role. In one of our most helpful approaches to the
quandary, each student has attempted to sum up his or her
gifts and interests with a metaphor for ministry. We have
then discussed these metaphors as organizing motifs for
ordering all the demands of the work. We have of course
used traditional images: prophet, teacher, herald, priest,

shepherd. But we have used others as well: artist, historian, coach, sheepdog. "Moral counselor" can be one more clarifying expression for pastoral identity.

The brightest color in the warp, as most readers will quickly recognize, is the mood of our times. We are struggling for a moral vision in our society; that struggle is echoed in a dissatisfaction with the inherited ethos in pastoral theology. For me the thread showed up in the fabric with the reading of a little book by psychologist Paul Pruyser, *The Minister as Diagnostician,* and then a theological book by Don Browning, *The Moral Context of Pastoral Care.* I am indebted to them. Both books have been helpful also to students preparing for ordained ministry.

I must acknowledge a debt of gratitude as well to James Gustafson, an unknowing mentor of mine for many years. He lectured a group of us practical theology professors in 1982 on the theme "The Minister as Moral Counselor."

Finally, as I indicate in my dedication, I am grateful to my students. In particular, I would cite the two seminars of students whose patient and energetic reflection on the moral counselor has contributed to these pages in subtle ways. They represent a long procession of students who have taught and nurtured me year after year. Among other things, seminaries, like churches, are caring communities of learners.

Contents

CHAPTER ONE

Perspective

*M*ARK *JONES, PASTOR OF ST. ANDREW'S* Church, makes a routine hospital call on Linda Philby, a parishioner. During a lull in their brief conversation, Linda blurts out, "What do you think about divorce?"

At this moment, a wide and complex range of concerns will guide Mark's pastoral action. Mark moves within a "field," like a magnetic field, with many magnets exerting force, shaping his action.

One set of forces in the field relates to Linda's meaning in asking the question. Mark knows the possibilities. Linda may be changing the subject, away from something painful—they were just talking about the need for surgery and the risks involved. He knows she may be wondering about the shaky marriage of her sister. She may be thinking about a friend who is having an affair, or simply about the rising divorce rate as reported in the newsmagazine on her nightstand. But Mark has to wonder, suddenly, about Linda's own marriage, too.

Linda may be morally troubled, or intellectually curious. She may want to know about one gospel's prohibition of divorce and another's grudging toleration of it; she may not know any biblical text on the matter at all. She may want to know what the church tradition now teaches, or what her friends in the congregation would think were she to separate from her husband, Nick. She may want moral support from Mark, support for a liberating step out of an oppressive or violent marriage, or firm guidance toward faithful perseverance in a less-than-perfect match.

Moreover, Mark knows that part of the "field" that shapes his action inevitably involves his own experience and history. It involves, perhaps, his lingering reaction to his own parents' divorce, and his sense of loss and guilt when it happened. It involves his own accumulated wisdom from his ministry with divorcing couples. Mark knows he needs to acknowledge these forces within himself and then hold back, letting his pastoral action be shaped not by generalizations but by this particular encounter with Linda, here and now, in this hospital room, and by prayerful openness to her and to that third party to any truly pastoral conversation, the divine presence.

Mark's "field" also includes an awareness of his role as a counselor. He asks himself questions that derive from canons of good professional practice and from his calling to be leader in the community of faith. At this point Mark experiences some tension. Will his action be determined exclusively by standards of good personal counseling—helping Linda "work through" her marital problems, if there are some, toward the end that her life might be the happiest and most fulfilling possible? Or does Mark as pastor and churchman have other concerns that appropriately come into play?

Mark knows that in overt and in hidden ways, he and the church represent a moral conscience within the community, suggesting goals and norms other than "happiness" and "fulfillment." He and the church use other language, about faithfulness to a faithful God, about the will of God, about altruistic love of the neighbor—"even the least," about the "law of Christ." How does this relate to Linda's question, Mark asks himself. Does he have an obligation to raise issues of right or wrong within the bounds of this pastoral care? And the broader question: To what extent does Linda need to discover a deeper moral and spiritual foundation for her life if she is to solve her immediate marital difficulties? The tension remains.

Mark's "field" includes concern for third parties—for Nick, the husband; for Cheryl and Danny, Nick and Linda's children.

It includes a concern for the maintenance of family life in the society at large—and also a caveat that in some instances this urgent, legitimate interest *can* become an oppressive idol restricting rather than furthering human welfare.

Mark's "field" includes theological concerns. How does *he* read the creation story and the gospels on man and woman, on marriage and promise-making, on marital failure and renewal, on personal freedom and fulfillment? What weight does he give to church tradition, to church law?

Mark is being called on to be a moral counselor, and many forces bear on this aspect of his work.

One Vantage Point

What does it mean to consider the minister as moral counselor? In the chapters ahead, I use this perspective to provide insight for our pastoral work. We learned as children that the Christian faith is an ethical monotheism. God cares about how the human community shapes its moral relationships. Our Christian sensibilities have much more than a simply ritualistic or sacerdotal shape to them. We not only celebrate the Word in worship; we also act it out in personal and communal life, in moral action.

Scripture undergirds this moral dimension of faith with both law and gospel, from the Ten Commandments and the prophets to the Sermon on the Mount and the young church's practical theology reflected in the epistles. The Bible is full of history and parable, of precept and counsel with moral implications.

Because of this behavioral dimension to Christian faith, we inevitably encounter the moral realm in the midst of our ministry. How best to help people grow in the moral life is the focus of this book.

Important as this dimension of pastoral leadership is, however, we must avoid reducing ministry to this single role. We are looking at ministry through but one lens, from one perspective.

No one viewpoint is exhaustive for examining a bit of reality. I say of a stone: It is marble (geology). It fits well here in the garden (landscaping and aesthetics). It speaks to me of creation (theology). It would be useful for a statue of David (art and craft). All these can be true of the stone at one and the same time.

The same may be said of ordained ministry. Actual pastoral ministry will remain itself beyond all that we say as we examine, describe, and reflect upon it—as a theologian may, for example, or a sociologist, a psychologist, an economist, a historian. None of these perspectives wholly "gets inside" ministry, which remains itself, intimately involved with the community's worship, its telling of the old, old story, its caring *diakonia* and *koinonia,* and its ordering and liberating of individual and social life.

Moral counseling is one essential perspective, then, but not the only one. Ethicists are tempted to reduce the Great Commandment's love of God (Mark 12:29-31 and par.) to its moral substance, to love of neighbor (cf. Outka, 1972, pp. 215-20). But the scheme of "two tables" in the Decalogue— the one on Godward, religious obligation, the other on ethics, is more our invention than that of ancient Israel. The biblical authors saw religious and moral obligation as one.

Nonetheless, the two separate clauses in the great commandment help clarify our thinking. So too do the traditions of the contemplatives, and the daily experience of our twin "service"—in worship and in work, Sunday and weekday, in enjoying God and in glorifying and serving God. The two elements are to be kept profoundly intertwined, however. The tradition prevents us from reducing the first one simply to the other.

The second commandment must exist within the first; we love the neighbor in our loving of God, because the neighbor is the beloved of God. The second is not to compete with the first. All our energy is to go into the love of God ("With *all* your heart, mind, soul, strength"). But the second must be present, or the love of God is scurrilous, fraudulent, or even idolatrous. The reason is simple. Lacking neighbor-love, godward religious deference is the worship of some god other than Israel's God of justice, mercy, and righteousness.

I stress both parts of the Great Commandment lest the emphasis on moral counsel lead us into a trap of legalism or callow activism, a life lacking roots in personal spirituality and the corporate church. Christian faith guides us in a life more fundamentally marked by freedom than by law, whether most people in the pews or in the traditional church can articulate that or not. To use but one striking remark, in this case from Carl Braaten, quoted by Paul Minear: "The dominant picture of God in western orthodoxy, whether Roman or Protestant, has been as the foremost advocate of law and order. . . . A religion of law and order is the cult of Caesar; when it is carried into the church it becomes the tyranny of the AntiChrist" (Minear, 1977, p. 86). Minear at this point is commenting on Galatians 6:14, particularly the words "the world has been crucified to me, and I to the world." The Christ-event ends the tyranny of the principalities, powers that include the world's concerns for the "flesh" and graceless, brittle law. "For neither circumcision counts for anything, nor uncircumcision, but a new creation" (Gal. 6:15).

All that having been said, however, the covenant community, once aware of God's gift of deliverance from old bondages, earnestly proceeds with the works of love. It becomes a community of moral concern and discourse. (In traditional language, these efforts fall not under the theological rubric of justification, but of sanctification, the "what then?" stage of the Christian life.) Lacking this moral aftermath, we must question whether "faith" is genuine or a self-deluding escape of some sort, whether it is the worship of the God of the prophets and of Jesus, or of some fiction. As Bonhoeffer puts it, "Only the believing obey; only the obedient believe."

Metaphors for Ministry

"Moral counselor" is both a lens for examining one aspect of ministry, and a metaphor that offers insights into the whole of our work. The use of metaphor prevents reductionism; it makes a more modest claim than an analytical formula. Yet it may at the same time offer a more creative avenue of thought. The "reflective practitioner" uses "generative metaphors" for problem-solving, says Donald Schön (1983, pp. 184-87). They provide us a new way of working a puzzle. Schön illustrates by telling a story of engineers assigned the task of designing paint-brushes with synthetic bristles, which function differently from the old natural-bristled ones. They solved their stubborn problem by thinking of a brush as a pump!

We stimulate reflection on the nature and purpose of the church with metaphors. In its relation to the world, for example, the church may be thought about as herald, as spiritual caregiver, as retreat, as pioneer, as revolutionary cadre, as moral teacher. Each metaphor offers different insights and presents different problems; each begs different biblical and theological perspectives to warrant it. Paul Minear discusses ninety-six biblical metaphors for the church, "images" like leaven, salt, Christ's body, new Israel (Minear, 1960).

In terms of the ordained minister, many possibilities present themselves. We may at one moment use an anthropological insight, for example, and consider the minister as a shaman. We then note roles all clergy serve as they express and mediate the "holy" for believers and worshipers. For better or worse, people tend to see the priest-minister-shaman as someone different, with powers to heal or bless, with special access to a spiritual realm (cf. Holmes, 1971, pp. 249-64).

Likewise, we may think of the minister as "coach," using an athletic metaphor. The minister trains the congregation for mission. This generative metaphor, like others, juxtaposes apparently inconsistent concepts and thereby provides new insight.

Students have given me insightful essays on the minister as artist, as exegete, as storyteller, and as historian, integrating the multifarious activities of the pastor around such organizing themes, and following the theme into newly suggested byways of understanding. Writers for the theological community have treated the minister as politician (Gustafson, 1969), as prophet (Shelp and Sunderland, 1985), as evangelist (Armstrong, 1984), and as resident theologian (Winter, 1963).

"Moral counselor," then, is one more generative metaphor for insight into the calling of the ordained minister, whether pastor of a congregation, chaplain in a hospital or school or regiment, denominational executive, teacher, or religious writer. The term *counselor* invites a number of word associations. It may remind us of the counselor-at-law, a now quaint term lawyers once used as they announced themselves to the public. It invites comparison with the work of psychotherapist and social case worker, to whom people go for "counseling." It suggests the work of the pastoral counselor, whose specialized ministry has drawn so heavily on the psychological disciplines.

Moral is an equally rich, not to say ambiguous, term. In common use, it has primarily to do with right behavior, with ethics and obligation. However, it is actually a more general term, referring also to personal character; it stands in contrast, for example, to the *physical* and *intellectual* aspects of human nature. We may speak of a moral victory, or moral support. The word has to do with the mind and human feeling. For the sociologist, it also points to human relations; a writer may contrast the moral community with the economic or the political community. Our reference to moral counselors will draw primarily on the first of all these possibilities, but overtones from the others will be heard as well.

Questions for Leadership

In using "moral counselor" as either standpoint or metaphor, we uncover a host of important questions bearing on leadership in the Christian community. How much ethical indoctrination, if any, is called for? How do we couple autonomy in moral reflection with disciplined adherence to the church's communal norms? What kinds of religious-moral norms shall the church espouse, and who, in that question, speaks for "the church"? Indeed, what is the place of anything like a moral code within the church's primary calling to proclaim the gospel, to tell the story of God? What is the authority of biblical moral precepts? And of which ones? How broad a pluralism of private, conscientious—and not so conscientious—moral and ethical life-styles shall the church intentionally include, or tolerate? When and how should the church discipline its members? How is the moral dimension of faith best mediated to adults, youth, and children, and to the society in which the church's mission is set? How does the church serve as moral resource to the broader culture?

These questions do not have simple answers, and many of them easily go beyond the scope of this work. In the following chapters, we shall look at ministry style and responsibility, touching on the broader questions as appropriate and as necessary. I address, in the next chapter, the issue of personal freedom and commitment. I must also attempt a brief statement of moral goals in the Christian life, without expanding the statement into a book on Christian ethics. We can then proceed with discussions of individual moral counsel, moral education, and other specific areas of the pastor's work.

An Urgent Matter

I have several reasons for this study. For one thing we need to move beyond our psychological preoccupations in pastoral care. I have long been convinced that personal well-being comes about indirectly. It is more the by-product of objective concern for the good of others than of a driving subjective quest for personal happiness. Such a conviction raises many objections to the temper of our age, variously described, by Philip Rieff as a time that experiences "the triumph of the therapeutic," by Christopher Lasch as a time of rampant narcissism. Calling us "moral counselors" picks up the image of psychological helpfulness but moves it off its subjective center, suggesting a unique role for pastors in counseling, teaching, and leadership.

Thomas Oden has written under a title that sums up this concern well: *After Therapy What?* If, through therapy and counseling, a person's life comes to be relatively free of internal conflict and fear, what then? Actually, my argument goes further than such a query. It asks whether it is not the case that, in the long run at least, healing and wholeness may not more likely result from shifting our perspective in pastoral care. Do we not need to move away from the self-centeredness of so much in counseling onto broader ground that still includes concern for the self, a perspective with a more "objective" preoccupation? That is no easy question. The parishioner seeking counsel is usually preoccupied with internal conflicts, unable to see beyond them. The pathway to healing requires a clearing of this undergrowth, not a lecture in morals. Yet the question persists. Does the turning away from self to neighbor come only after some threshold of health is reached, or is there need for that perspective all along the way?

Conversion, problematic a word as it is, points to that kind of turning, whether traumatic and sudden or only once-born and healthy-minded, to use William James' words. The moral counselor wants to help a person move toward grounding a life in God and putting it to God's service. The moral counselor believes this route is the way toward health.

The pastoral arts made immense gains during the earlier decades of this century as we took account of the new therapeutic disciplines after Freud and James and Rogers. The excitement was such, however, that pastoral counseling, modeled after a secular psychological discipline rather than our own tradition of the cure of souls, often came to be a dominant paradigm for the whole of ministry. The kerygmatic edge of ministry was blunted by such a vision, helpful as the pastoral caregivers were for thousands upon thousands of persons who sought out the supportive and healing listeners in the pastor's office. Calling the minister *moral* counselor may, while acknowledging the gains rather than rejecting them, help in the shift toward a more comprehensive and better focused understanding of ministry. It also allows a better integration of other roles such as the educational and "public" ministry that are part of the pastor's work.

Second, I believe this emphasis in ministry is theologically urgent. Spiritual integrity demands moral integrity. Blessing God means sharing blessings with the neighbor. If we do not love our neighbor, whom we have seen, we cannot love God. Yet for many well-meaning Christians and their clergy, faith has come to mean good religious feeling in a self-centered suburban world, or right-believing in a brittle evangelicalism, equally self-centered. In either case both individual lives and the human community are short-changed by their parish leadership. The moral counselor metaphor will help us deepen and broaden our perspective on our work. Too many local congregations ignore or tiptoe around important Christian matters because they have not learned from any counselor-at-ethics the gist of faithful and reflective moral action.

Finally, we need in these years of our society's history all the moral reflection we can come by. If the church is to fulfill its time-honored role of being a significant goad and partner in that reflection, its pastors must serve as counselors-at-ethics in the congregation. We have had enough of leaving it to the secular technicians and experts, as if the Pentagon would be self-motivating enough toward disarmament, or the best and the brightest (Halberstam, 1972) would keep us out of Vietnam. I will say more about the dangers present when the minister or the church claims to be the moral arbiter for others or for the culture, but the need for looking at ministry leadership in this perspective is apparent with every daily newscast.

Oden, in *After Therapy What?* affirms his increasing skepticism about the professionalization of so much therapy, and he celebrates the explosion of therapeutic relationships into lay-led support groups of many sorts. Similarly, enhancing and expanding the arenas of moral reflection and action in our society becomes the larger goal of the "moral counselor."

CHAPTER TWO

Groundworks
for the Moral
Counselor

THE MOST USEFUL THEOLOGICAL REFLECTION takes place in dialogue with practice. We do not travel a one-way street from religious philosophy to current practice. We practice theology in the living faith community, in light of its pain and passion as well as its professed and inherited belief. Beginning with the next chapter, the dialogue of praxis will guide us in fleshing out the moral dimension of the minister's work. At this point, however, I offer some general comments about the foundations on which our work as moral counselors must rest.

Human life, in the Christian view, is called into being by a purposeful God. Human destiny is fulfilled in our affirmative response to God, by our acceptance of God's merciful and transforming love toward us. The nature of this response has been understood in many different ways. The emphasis has changed from one time to another, and from one tradition to another. At one time it may be personal piety; at another asceticism, or loyalty to the institutional church, or individual confession and conversion. At still others the most salient emphasis may be work and service, societal change and liberation, or liturgical, sacramental worship. Whatever the emphasis, for the sake of its life and mission the community calls forth and trains up leadership in the several theological tasks: interpreting the biblical sources and the story of Jesus for each successive generation; probing human experience in light of the story; nurturing corporate religious life and that of individual Christians; helping the community toward Christian action in the world. This leadership task relates us to such fundamental moral concerns as human freedom, commitment, the search for happiness, and altruistic love.

Freedom

Let us say that Linda Philby comes to Mark with a seemingly firm conviction. She wants a divorce from Nick. Unless he has talked at length with Linda before, there are profound reasons that Mark as a conscientious pastor cannot simply say "I understand," and let it go at that. We have suggested something of the range of these reasons in chapter 1.

There are equally strong reasons why Mark will not simply exert his clerical authority and say, "But that's wrong!" The reasons go beyond those clustering around the obvious need for deeper insight into Linda's meaning and her situation. They have to do with personal freedom and autonomy.

In order for a course of action to qualify as "moral," it must take place in freedom. If I cannot do other than deed A because of either external coercion or irresistible inner compulsion, if, that is, there are no alternatives, then doing deed A is not really a decision. The confession given under threat of torture, for example, is not admitted to court as an authentic, moral statement. The small child, who as yet lacks the reflective competence to weigh alternatives of whether to behave well or misbehave, is not held "morally" accountable. If Linda, somehow so enraptured by the authority Mark has as pastor or by the teaching authority of the church, slavishly, "compulsively," and without even acknowledging the possibility of divorce in a society like ours, stays married for the *sole* reason of this coercive dictation by external authority, she is not making a fully moral decision. Nor, of course, does she have much of a marriage!

The time-worn question of the freedom of the will is ever new in ethical discussion. In our freedom, none of us is altogether free of outside pressures or internal determinants. All manner of forces bear in upon a weighty decision—persuasive and partially coercive pressures from other people, from rules and customs, from attractive alternatives, from vectors of past habit and the momentum of promises made; such elements compose the raw material of moral choice. As Linda and Nick consider the possibility of marital failure, many factors come into play: the church's teaching, societal norms, the present emotional quality of their relationship, the vows undertaken at marriage, the lives of the children, the degree of realism in hoping for reconciliation. Mark Jones can attempt to dictate a decision. If he should succeed, to the extent that it is his decision and not that of Linda and Nick, it lacks moral integrity.

The moral counselor cannot be simply an authoritarian moral arbiter, a decider for others, without destroying the very moral end in view, the maturity of the moral agent seeking counsel.

Counselors know two other reasons, of course, why they do not make decisions *for* clients or parishioners. In the first place, it doesn't work. Until decisions are made "from inside," until they are the decisions of the parishioner rather than mere acts of compliance with the strictures of others, those decisions are not likely to endure.

In the second place, the counselor can never know as much about the entire situation in which the moral effort must be exerted as can the parishioner personally. Some years ago Chief Justice Earl Warren of the Supreme Court suggested that clergy become "moral counselors" to business and professional people in light of the heavy ethical decisions they have to make. If his idea is thought to have meant that right moral answers could be handed out by clerical moral experts, it was all wrong. It would imply that the lawyer and the judge, the business manager and the physician, the teacher and the architect are not more apt, once they come to moral consciousness, to make better decisions in their places of work and policy formation, than the theologian. The counselor, far from dictating day-by-day decisions, can but assist the laity in their own vocation to be faithful.

Commitment over Time

This stress on personal freedom does not mean that conscientious action takes place in a vacuum, an existentialist's void, apart from vectors of moral influence. We have to consider not only the multiple obligations to others in the present but also obligations incurred in the past, for the present. Freedom does not consist of solipsistic private decisions made in isolated, instant moments, unrelated to other moments, past and future. One of the chief elements in the moral life is the promise or the vow, in which we yield to others, as Margaret Farley puts it, a claim on our freedom for some future time (1986, p. 16). The moral counselor helps people deal with these claims, often troublesome because of new claims that arise, or new desires that conflict with old promises.

The agent of moral action is the person, the self, which has continuity with the past and with the future. Human time is not like the moment-by-moment instants of a digital watch, ostensibly obliterating the previous moment each second a new figure is presented. In the sweep of human time, past and future involve themselves intimately in the present moment. The mix of tenses helps constitute the self.

Forgetting either past or future leaves us less than whole. Take away a person's memory, and we have left only a potential person. Take away all hope, and we have an organism in despair, probably soon to die. The Christian lives on a wide, wide stage, and the backdrop brings past and future actively to that scene. Christians live "between the times" because we respond to God's actions in the past and to the promise of divine sustenance in times ahead.

The present is alive with more than spirit. It is alive with memory and with hope as well. It is the failure of some of our new age thinking that it forgets the past and shucks off commitment. "Live in the moment," it says, and it is a very narrow moment.

Linda and Nick's marriage can founder with too narrow a moment in mind. The present is miserable, says one party or the other. He or she may then discard the couple's past and their future in what later may turn out to have been a mistaken panic.

Memory without the yearning forward would leave us mere antiquarians, researching dusty manuscripts. We would lack the purposeful use of the past for the shaping of a world. But losing that and concentrating only on the future would leave us in an unseasoned, adolescent, quixotic adventurism, conducive neither to mental health nor social survival in a nuclear age.

We still hear talk about contextual ethics, an ethics according to the present situation. But so much bears on the situation! The Christian who includes in the context of decision the grand tapestry of God's story—past, present, and future—finds the moral calculus transformed.

Over time, then, the moral life evolves, not only setting limits for the decisions of any moment, but also, and more important, giving these decisions foundations of habit and character that make of the self more than a will-of-the-wisp, giving it moral substance and strength for making moral choices. Part of the very meaning of selfhood is in undertaking commitments. Making a promise seems to bind future moments and restrict their freedom, but it is the very stuff of many of our moral concerns. Often this is an explicit act—striking a bargain, signing a contract, pledging allegiance, plighting troth. Often too, however, it is not. It simply grows up as an understanding—commitments to a family or a community, to friends, to children.

Parishioners bring a variety of concerns in relation to their commitments. How long should a promise be honored? Does it stand over and against our present freedom? What justifies breaking a promise? The questions can come with great specificity. How do *we* counsel Linda, or Linda and Nick, who have made a vow, "till death do us part?" What is the promise made to a parent, and what is the better way to "honor father and mother," when that parent needs either to move in with a son or daughter a thousand miles from the old homestead, or be placed in a nursing home close to many friends?

The tendency of academic ethics to focus on the hard decision, and the ambiguous situation, should not blind us to the fundamental fact that moral life is far more than a matter of character than one of exercising cognitive competence in the midst of ethical quandaries. Character, like promises, comes from the past and conditions decisions of the present. A person may say, in face of a temptation to lie or cheat: "It's not really a decision, at all. I could have done no other than what I did and still remain true to myself." In this sense, what was said about Linda above could be misleading. If she simply never considers divorce because, difficult as her marriage is, in the nature of her own character, divorce "doesn't occur to her," as she might put it, that is quite different from external coercion. Linda's embeddedness in the marriage results from a moral quality of her life.

The Paradox in Seeking Happiness

The most commonplace basis for motivation and persuasion, the one used by advertiser and T.V. evangelist alike, is the search for personal happiness. We are urged to buy, to read, to taste, to view, and even to believe because it will be of benefit to us; it will make us happier. This pitch is ubiquitous, and one might well ask, "What other ground of appeal can there be?" It is universal, and so the egoistic ethicist will assume a priori that every act is a search for personal benefit. Such a theorist will force even the most disinterested act of love or service into that single mold. The person who risks life and limb, for example, to save a drowning stranger or a child straying into the path of an oncoming truck is said to be seeking recognition as a hero or to be avoiding otherwise inevitable guilt. There can be no selfless act.

That there are other ways of putting the case for moral effort is an assumption of religious faith. Much as we know the mix of self-seeking that is in all of us, we know the reality of loyalty and service to God of a sort that takes us out of ourselves, beyond self-seeking. God is beyond us. We can visualize serving God at cost even to life itself, the very opposite of self-seeking. Jesus, of course, reiterates this paradox. We are to lose life if we are to gain it.

The structuring of thought about the moral response to God takes various forms. One form stresses obedience, doing God's will, cultivating the virtues God enjoins. "What does the Lord require?" a person asks. Precedents for deontological ethics abound. The God of the decalogue was a law-giving God, providing the way, the torah, for a good life and a good society. Likewise, the New Testament suggests to us norms like the "law of love" in the great commandment, or the ethical injunctions in Romans 12.

Another form of expression builds on our vision, our yearning for a better life for the race. It too is a deeper and broader quest than the search for private personal happiness. One of our social gospel hymns goes, "These things shall be: a loftier race/Than e'er the world hath known shall rise/With flame of freedom in their souls/And light of knowledge in their eyes" (John A. Symonds, "These Things Shall Be"). Moral effort in this case stems from the vision of the good. Formal ethics speaks of the utilitarian school, with its dominant question in decision-time about what will accomplish in the long run the most good for the most people. Fraught with difficulty as it is—such as defining "good" in that very sentence—there is plenty of religious precedent for this future-oriented stance. Both the old and the new Israel reach out in their communal pilgrimages and their moral life toward the kingdom, the shalom-blessed community.

Yet a third way of thinking about grounding the moral life stresses gratitude and a less rule-oriented or future-oriented response to the moral universe. In our experience some people do quite spontaneously affirm others at cost to themselves, without a primary emphasis on either obligation or the long-run good. For Christians, emphasis on response to God's gracious love plays a central role in understanding motivation. We are free from law, we say.

The traditions of law represent guidance, but we move beyond legalism. We know a richer moral life than what is afforded by trying to measure out all future good, much as the symbol of God's coming realm inspires us. H. Richard Niebuhr, in *The Responsible Self,* championed this third emphasis as the basis of the Christian's moral life. We are to act out the fitting or appropriate response to the self-disclosing graciousness of God.

Letting go of law and kingdom, of course, threatens to usher us toward too lax a Christian style. Dietrich Bonhoeffer calls it "cheap grace" when we stress God's saving action without a sense of the cost of discipleship (1963). His writing shows how important is attending to the God who truly is, as best we can know, rather than a sugar-coated God of our projected wishes, if we are to think through our ethics in this liberating but risky Christian style.

On what ground do we stand? In the midst of decision-making, it is quite natural to ask, of ourselves or of a parishioner, "Which way do you think you will be happiest?" We need to remind ourselves of the fact, however, that this is only one kind of query. Of itself, it begs a host of questions. Is happiness best sought so directly? Is happiness the deepest human need? Is happiness to be bought by a self-concern that ignores the happiness of others? What do we make of the scriptural injunctions about *not* seeking for self but seeking first God's realm, laying down one's life, going a second mile, of cherishing the neighbor's good rather than one's own?

The quest for happiness presents a paradox. As we move beyond self-preoccupation, we also become richer selves, discovering that we have won our happiness without seeking it. The experience comes to parents, lovers, saints who leave behind wealth and family ties, and artists and researchers for whom the "other" is less a person than objective beauty or truth to which they dedicate themselves. The ultimate in this paradox, of course, is to be found when we acknowledge, strangely, that someone's integrity and joy were affirmed even in martyrdom.

Abraham Maslow has presented a well-known systematic

scale of human needs that supposedly traces our human quest. The basic needs of sustenance and security come first and then others such as social affiliation. The scale culminates in self-realization. Even Maslow, however, admits to finding another perspective in the "self-realized" group. Avoiding religious language as a psychological scientist, he pointed to the dedication he found in this group of people, who so fascinated him. We also might conclude that they seem quite different from self-seeking persons who have set out to "actualize" themselves!

Our subjects are in general strongly focused on problems outside themselves. In current terminology, they are problem centered rather than ego centered. . . . These individuals customarily have some mission in life, some task to fulfill, some problem outside themselves which enlists much of their energies. This is not necessarily a task that they would prefer or choose for themselves; it may be a task that they feel is their responsibility, duty, or obligation. . . . In general these tasks are nonpersonal or unselfish, concerned rather with the good of mankind in general, or of a nation in general, or of a few individuals in the subject's family. (Maslow, 1954, p. 211)

"Happiness" is only a shallow answer to the question, What do you need? We need most of all to see our lives against a larger backdrop than a private pursuit of happiness. In Viktor Frankl's term, our need is for *meaning* in our lives—whether they be comfortable or burdened by suffering (1963). Paul Tillich argued that the modern form of sin—of alienation from God—is an oppressive sense of meaninglessness (Tillich, 1952, pp. 32-63).

All this is to say that we do not get very far by asking a parishioner-counselee, "What will make you the happiest?" natural as the question is. That question can blind us to the need for faith-grounded moral strength and the roundabout patterns of fulfillment laid out in the paradox above. The happiness question in counseling is not necessarily a sellout, but it can be. The context within the pastoral conversation will suggest appropriate alternative responses or questions. "This restlessness keeps tormenting you."

(What does this restlessness stem from and mean to the parishioner?) "And you feel God wants something of you in the midst of this?" (What does the parishioner think of if we ask what God wants in all of this?) Or, "Recognizing that you are not alone in this decision, and that others are affected, what seems best to you?"

Self-Love and the Doormat Question

The responses just proposed turn the inquiry somewhat away from the self toward a broader canvas. But they do not dispose of the psychological need for self-regard. The other issue persists. Am I to be a doormat? What about my own happiness? What about self-love?

We have all heard many sermons, in church and out, exhorting us to love ourselves. They arise from pastoral encounters with people who suffer because they do not respect themselves, and from fascination with self-realization lingo. Although Jesus said nothing on record about those popular modern concepts self-acceptance and self-esteem (he said much about *God's* acceptance of us), these preachments often cite the second clause of the great commandment, "You shall love your neighbor as yourself." They claim that it means an obligation to oneself like what is touted by today's popular psychology. Far more logically, the commandment means that self-regard is a given, and that we should match that instinctive self-love with an equal dedication to the neighbor's well-being. Jesus does not dwell on self-love. He teaches agape, disinterested love, a selfless, compassionate concern for the neighbor that does not count the cost. For the psychologically conditioned and the unsaintly—that is, all of us—this raises the doormat question. Are we to let people walk all over us?

Gene Outka, in his survey of theological texts on selfless love, *Agape,* admits there is little consensus on the moral status of self-love (pp. 55-74). He catalogs four appraisals of it. For some theologians, self-love is wholly "nefarious," unworthy, to be confessed, and fought off. Others simply see it as normal, part of the furniture of life. A third group of writers justifies it as an element necessary for the sake of the larger good of the neighbor, using not psychological argument but ethical reasoning. Finally, some writers do affirm self-love as continuing moral obligation in its own right.

The pattern of reasoning in the third of these positions merits elaboration. At what point, and for what reasons, rather than laying down life for the neighbor, or going the second mile, do we assert ourselves? Agape, the argument goes, is suspicious of the self-deceiving rationalizations pervasive in self-love. It is serious about the dominant claim of the neighbor, which is taught in the gospels' radical law of love. But it is no "blank check." Outka suggests three instances when self-regard becomes important in neighbor-love (pp. 68-69). First, we must assert ourselves when failure to do so is bad for the neighbor, when, for example, such failure encourages the neighbor's corruption, or when it destroys rather than strengthens the stable, just, communal fabric of human life. Second, we may exert our power against the neighbor's will or need when third parties are involved, and when their injury may result from our "weakness" in deferring to the neighbor. Third, we may stand up for ourselves and seek our own welfare in order not to become a burden on others.

The parish minister knows of a host of psychological reasons for self-regard. Outka's sense of the need for appropriate self-assertion encompasses them. We have seen defeated, self-destructive parishioners who lack—in painfully large degree—self-acceptance, self-affirmation, self-esteem. We have seen parents who distort normal child-oriented parental self-sacrifice into a harmful permissiveness, or a destructive possessiveness. We have seen children who are too slow to develop a sense of their own competence and worthiness. As pastors, we want them all to know, as that most famous of Paul Tillich's sermons put it, that "you are accepted." Somehow, without urging them toward an overweening egoism, we want them to discover the strengths of self-esteem. We want them to enjoy the created selfhood they have been given by God, and to make their contribution to the human community. The selflessness enjoined upon us in the gospel notwithstanding, what both our experience and behavioral science point to is not irrelevant in meeting this need for personal strength. The "stronger" person has more to give the neighbor, if he or she but will.

The Difficulty and Virtue of the Medical Model

For good reason, our modern world has a love affair with science. Technology has solved too many problems and has enriched our understanding of the natural order too much for us to go back on science. Nonetheless, that there can be a technological fix for the deepest problems of the human soul and the human community is implausible.

Part of the difficulty experienced by the minister as moral counselor results from the attempt to take account of both behavioral science and the more intuitive truths that emerge from faith. This dilemma has taken particular shape in the pastoral counseling movement. Although it was probably inevitable, because of the cultural involvement with science, it is at least partly a historical accident that medicine and psychiatry came to be taken as the prototype of therapeutic agents for troubled persons rather than priesthood and ministry. As Thomas Oden once put it, "If the ministry or priesthood had not been burdened with quaint and archaic role expectations, it might have served as a more viable model than medicine" (1974, p. 4).

The psychiatrist is first trained in scientific medicine. Science by definition must stress objectivity. In the human "sciences" like psychology, and in the practice of psychotherapy, objectivity sometimes translates into a supposition that the therapist can treat patient or client from a "value-free" base.

Had Oden's fancy been served, and had priesthood become the model of therapy, a different framework might have undergirded soul-cure, psyche-healing. There would inevitably have been more implicit and explicit emphasis on a vision of the virtuous life, and, in the background, a stronger feel for the grounding of human interaction in the redemptive nature of things, or in God. Psychotherapy itself cannot proceed without something of that vision and that sense of health-giving forces, but grounded on "science," its envisioning is usually covert.

The traditions of priestly care include a richer kind of guidance than "value-free" professional relations. They are passionate, concerned, and engaged. In some of their ancient forms, they use imagery that cannot serve as therapeutic currency in the modern world. But pairings like sin and salvation, the demonic and the redemptive, self-seeking and Christ-centeredness, human despair and the power of God, represent a quality in the interpersonal encounter of pastor and parishioner that we can recover. It is a quality sadly lacking in pastoral conversation that defers too much to the psychological-science, medical, and psychiatric models.

We may quote now from one of the radicals in psychiatry, without meaning to imply an approval of all his work by any means. Thomas Szasz argued as follows:

In actual practice, [psychiatrists] deal with personal, social, and ethical problems in living. . . . The notion of a person "having a mental illness" is scientifically crippling. It provides professional assent to a popular rationalization, namely, that problems in human living . . . are significantly similar to *diseases of the body*. It also undermines the principle of personal responsibility . . . by assigning to an external source [i.e., the "illness"] the blame for antisocial behavior. (*The Myth of Mental Illness*, Thomas Szasz [New York: Dell, 1961, pp. 296-97] [quoted in Oden, 1974, p. 6])

If, in practice, therapists "deal with personal, social, and ethical problems in living," how much more the clergy.

These have been strong statements, perhaps overly dramatic. Psychiatry is, as Szasz says, deeply humane in practice. And there *are* outside intruders, and there *are* medical remedies to treat them, in mental illness as in other diseases. The half emptying of our larger state mental hospitals beginning with the introduction of chlorproma-zine in the late '50s demonstrated that. My point is that soul-care is not a monopoly of medical and psychiatric science, and that "the principle of responsibility," a moral matter, is a concern of the minister as moral counselor.

The ambiguity in our understanding of this kind of human anguish may be seen more clearly, perhaps, if we look at one of the most common of human problems in parish life, alcoholism. We gain considerable advantage by considering alcoholism a disease. Yet in another perspective the problem is, in the broadest sense of the word, moral.

Most experts on alcoholism assert straightforwardly, "Alcoholism is a disease." There are advantages in the label, and an approach to alcoholism under this label is the most successful. "Objections to calling alcoholism a disease usually stem from the fact that we tend to construe the term 'disease' too narrowly," says one counselor (Royce, 1985, p. 503). "[Alcoholism] must be understood as a physiological, psychological, and spiritual illness: the whole person is sick." There is even evidence that heredity, aside from social and familial environment, plays a role in alcoholism (50 percent of the children of alcoholic parents become alcoholics themselves), and there may yet be firm physiological evidence that "the alcoholic's liver and brain react differently to alcohol than other people's" (Royce, 1985, p. 508).

Nonetheless, using "disease" for alcoholism is as much a metaphor as a diagnosis. It establishes a perspective; it does not write a drugstore prescription. Some alcoholics need medical attention for their ailments, but the effective "treatment" of most alcoholism is not an antibiotic injection, a pill, or a hospital bed. It is a communal, moral process, participation in Alcoholics Anonymous, in which a person is both supported *and* challenged to assume responsibility for his or her behavior of drinking. The AA group provides an intimate, sharing group. The alcoholic's denials are shot down. The twelve steps of AA deal with guilt, humility, and forgiveness. They refer, with a spiritual emphasis, to a "Higher Power," and, in step eleven, to "prayer and meditation." AA does not give out pharmaceutical drugs. Except in those few cases where it is in a clinic, the AA meeting consists of a lay-led group. AA is not moralistic. It does not focus on judgmental discipline for wayward "sinners." But it is unquestionably a process of moral counsel. And it helps. One Rand Corporation long-term study of more than nine hundred alcoholics showed that AA participation increased one's chance of remaining abstinent by 32 to 47 percent, regardless of other therapy of any sort, or none at all. No other therapies are so widespread and can claim a similar record (Andrews, 1987, p. 154).

While the debate about the appropriateness of the medical label for alcoholism continues, we in the church have much to learn from the way that this "disease" perspective helps the alcoholic. For one thing, because of it, alcoholics are far less likely to be stereotyped as skid-row bums and put out of mind. (Only 3 percent of alcoholics fit that image.) They are less likely to be jailed without further help. Furthermore, there is a nonjudgmental objectivity to this kind of diagnosis. It helps overcome denial. It is far easier for a person to admit to a disease than to a moral fault.

Most of all, however, calling alcoholism a disease undercuts moralism and its enormous pitfalls. When the alcoholic comes to the AA meeting and hears that alcoholism is a disease, he or she says, "Thank God! It's not a condition of moral turpitude. I have an affliction." That experience for the alcoholic is like receiving a word of grace. Condemnation is past; judgment is withdrawn. The alcoholic at last experiences firm, concerned acceptance.

What keeps so many alcoholics away from church is the moralistic judgment of others upon them. The church is itself a group of sinners, all of us suffering a disease. If this were only to sink in deeply, we of the church could give expression much more effectively to the grace of God. Our moralism would be displaced. We would have for the world a message like that of AA for the alcoholic: "You are accepted. We have a disability like yours. If we are able, let us help you with your struggle."

We too need to be saying, "Everyone here in this community of faith suffers. Everyone struggles with his or her own problems of sin." (The word *sin* itself now has such moralistic connotations that it is nearly unusable.) "We want to be of help to others with the same afflictions. So you too are sick. Let us tell you our experience. With our help, and God's, you will be able to cope." AA, the alcoholic will report to us, is a supportive fellowship, even while holding its firm convictions of method and of the need for abstinence. This is a serious-minded moral community. The testimonies, the stories of despair and courage, are shared. "It's like this with me, and probably for you." But there is an absence of high-handed moralizing, of judgmental posturing.

We can learn from all that. The moral counselor cannot succeed by dishing out moral advice as judgment. The theological warning is clear. "If thou, O Lord, shouldst mark iniquities, Lord, who could stand?" (Ps. 130:3). The moral counselor, like the Samaritan, gets down into the ditch to bind up the wounds. In Nouwen's apt phrase, the minister is a wounded healer, who uses the personal experience of affliction to better serve others in their affliction.

Moralism and Moral Concern

Just as self-righteous piety is a shadow in the formal practice of religion, moralism is a shadow connected to morality. Moralism is ethics without depth, without soul. It is the reduction of ethics to rules and preachments, without a true sense of the good, the true, and the beautiful. It is morality without human empathy.

The codification of morality is an ambiguous enterprise. History and the evolution of language present us with stereotypes that represent virtue turned sour by moralistic excess—the Pharisee, the Puritan. They also show us movements that have fostered personal ethics and yet lacked the wider social compassion and vision indispensable to true moral concern. One thinks of Moral Rearmament, Opus Dei, the Latin Cursillo movement. Such movements have helped many people pull their lives together. Yet they are subject to a deeper moral critique. Puritanism provided a moral backbone for the American culture; its emphases on honesty, diligence, and "this-worldly asceticism" influence even yet some of the best trends in economic, political, and social life. Yet rebellion against the stereotype comes from moral concern as well.

The good moral counselor, therefore, will always be alert to the shadow of moralism that can corrupt virtue. That means the counselor is more interested in intentions than in rules of conduct, more interested in disposition toward the neighbor than in technical ethical quandaries. The pastoral task of moral counsel lacks the crisp clarity of a manual on correct procedures in automobile repair. Personal moral development involves mainly emotion and the human will, much as it needs clear thinking. These elements will crop up over and over in our discussion of the minister as moral counselor.

CHAPTER THREE

The Moral Counselor
in Pastoral Care

MOST OFTEN, PEOPLE DO NOT COME TO THEIR pastors asking for explicit moral advice. Few of their troubles spring from clear-cut ethical dilemmas. Here is a sampling from one minister's record file in pastoral counseling, listing what people presented as their difficulties: a sense of drivenness; a sense of guilt—over broken relationships, in another case over feeling so much hate, in yet another case over being too self-centered; an inability to cope because of too many pressures; being depressed, feeling suicidal; experiencing marital problems—surfacing in quarreling, in (another case) sexual maladjustment, in (another) financial worry; difficulty in "handling" the children; suffering a sense of worthlessness; being bored with studies; being bored at work; being too indecisive; uncertainty about sexual orientation; loneliness and a hunger for affection; having a runaway teenage daughter; finding the premarital period difficult; doubting God's reality; wanting to reject the Bible; experiencing problems in prayer.

Linda Philby herself would probably say she wants help with a personal problem. She can feel that need in different ways. She may want sympathy. Or she may want strength to proceed with hard choices—a decision, perhaps, to work with Nick to strengthen their marriage, or to confront him with her desire for a divorce. Linda may simply be so lonely that she wants to talk with someone, someone other than Nick, who is far from the best listener on the block and who thinks "things are going along pretty well." Sympathy, emotional strength, an antidote to loneliness: These are undramatic, commonplace goals that bring people together in caring conversation, with their peers and with their pastors.

On occasion, of course, dramatic ethical crises do present themselves in the pastor's study. People bring heartrending questions about getting an abortion when amniocentesis discloses fetal handicaps in a new pregnancy; about the right course of action when the boss is falsifying reports to the stockholders; about premarital sex; about asking the doctor's assistance in helping Dad, now declining and experiencing intolerable pain, to die sooner. But most people come for help with concerns that do not appear to be so neatly related to ethics as all that. They bring "personal" problems.

The Moral Dimension

Nearly all the requests for help that come to pastors have their moral dimensions, nonetheless. Virtually all the difficulties listed by the pastor above admit of a moral component, in spite of the way our culture's *Zeitgeist* forces most of these parishioners to think of their problems—and us to perceive them—as psychological, at least on first view. In this chapter, to further our inquiry into pastoral method, we look at the goals of the moral counselor and at the pastor's region of service, the pastor's proper turf.

Whether done by a pastor or a psychotherapist, the enterprise of counseling represents moral endeavor. There is no such thing as "value-free" interpersonal encounter. To turn one's attention toward counseling as a way of helping others (instead, let us say, of carpentry or teaching school) is a value-laden choice made by the counselor. The motivation for the work has moral overtones. Is it for money, for personal satisfaction, for helping others? The way the counselee is regarded shapes the care pervasively. Is that person a "patient"? a "case"? a co-believer and parishioner? a child of God?

Moreover, the quality of that relationship has moral dimensions: the level of integrity or dissimulation in it, the level of congruence in language, affect and gesture; the desire of either party to manipulate the other, to dominate; and the degree of openness or hiddenness in both counselee and counselor. The goals for human life held by the therapist or caregiver inevitably affect the course of counsel. In all these ways there is a moral framework not only to pastoral care but to all secular care as well.

The goals of *pastoral* care go well beyond those of psychological adjustment and the solutions of such problems as intrapsychic ambivalence and interpersonal conflict. The nature and goals of pastoral care are variously defined. Eduard Thurneysen argues that pastoral care is little else than a specialized instance of preaching. Jacob Firet focuses on the New Testament word *paraklesis,* with its various meanings of exhortation and urgent invitation, and says pastoral care "addresses persons in their situations of need . . . with an eye to their being called to discipleship" (1986, p. 203). Don Browning looks at church history and sees a double role: incorporating members into the faithful community and its moral discipline, and assisting persons in various life crises. Over the last half-century, education for ministry has emphasized the latter at the expense of the former. Pastoral theology now seeks a better balance.

In broadest terms, the goal of pastoral care and of pastoral moral counsel is growth in faith. The same can be said of all pastoral leadership. That is to say, the goal is not in the first place conformity to some behavioral norm. We are midwives of maturation—maturation on the part of the parishioner, of the congregation and the wider church, and of the community—toward the kinds of human fulfillment implicit in the invitation-commandment to love God and love the neighbor. Our goal is to assist one another to live our personal and corporate life in light of a vision of the realm of God, the just and wholesome community, graced by God's sustaining presence and governance. Within that vision, we live both the joyful "as if" (as if we are already in the presence of the kingdom), and the engaged "so that" (so that something like God's rule may more easily come on earth).

Autonomy

In spite of the distinct religious perspective that has just been emphasized, the moral counselor can acknowledge considerable common ground with the secular counselor. We have initiated a discussion of autonomy in the previous chapter's emphasis on freedom. Whatever else the expressions mean, Christian conversion, becoming a "slave" to Christ (I Cor. 7:22), and "losing life for the sake of the gospel" (Mark 8:35) do not mean destruction of selfhood in the psychological sense, being "brainwashed" until one responds to the world mechanically and without authenticity. Disciplined a person may be, guided by virtuous habit until quite predictable in behavior, but the healthy person is engaged with his or her activities and interpersonal relations, not deadened like the drug-ridden person with the absent, blank stare. The person has emotion and feeling, spontaneity of action and of cognition. For the Christian, the God-relation is one of covenanted loyalty and love that provide identity rather than taking it away.

Concern for autonomy should hold a place equal to that of discipline as we raise children, lest enforcing confirmity to social norms destroy initiative in the child. First the child must possess a self; then moral engagement with the world is meaningful. In a "Peanuts" cartoon strip, strong-willed Lucy presents indecisive Charlie Brown with a two-kinds-of-people question. On a cruise ship, says Lucy, some people face their deck chairs to the stern, to see where they have been, and others face forward, to see where they are going. Which way would you set your chair, Charlie Brown? Charlie Brown has to think a while, and then he says, "I can't get my chair unfolded." One of our first moral goals is to help people get their chairs unfolded. Psychologists have taken note of that remarkable period in the very young child's life when the language of "me" shifts to "I." It is one more sign of the crucial emergence of the self.

In a sense, becoming Christian is like becoming human. As Christians we share with non-Christians in the culture a vision of the healthy person—blessed with emotional energy, a cognitive interest in the world, competence for interactive engagement with others, and self-acceptance. Whatever in moral counsel would take it away is wrong.

Such an affirmation appears to fly in the face of much in scripture and in other religious literature. Paul will catch himself up after describing some act of his own, and say: "No, not I, but Christ in me." Augustine writes about being not so much the archer aiming his own life, as the arrow being aimed. There is a paradox from mixing active and passive voice in Christian grammar. A young woman, feeling ambivalent about starting in a spiritual direction, expresses a hesitation that is fairly common: "Maybe I'll lose my personal identity," she says, "if I become fully used as a vessel of Christ" (Freeman, 1986, p. 39).

This paradox in the language of spirituality is hardly unique to religion. Does the musician lose "identity" or autonomy when caught up in the flow of the music? Yes, and no. In one sense that is the moment when the musician is most truly himself or herself. The language of faithful piety includes both "I . . ." and "Christ-in-me." Were the musician a victim of the music, never able to get outside it for ordinary living, always hearing it but never doing anything creative with it, we could say autonomy was lost. We can think of analogous examples of psychosis in religious garb.

Jacob Firet quotes from Brunner's dogmatics, "To be led by the spirit of God is not to be possessed. On the contrary, it is to be liberated from possession, from the alien domination of evil. Man only becomes himself through the operation of the Holy Spirit" (in Firet, 1986, pp. 124-25). Firet also reminds us of T. V. Adorno's studies of the authoritarian personality, born of concern over anti-Semitism and other prejudice. Prejudiced persons reported that they grew up in families that enforced fearful subservience to parental demands. The unprejudiced adult did not as a rule have to submit to stern authority in childhood. As a result there was less longing for strong authority or a need to assert one's strength against those who are weaker (p. 153). The enforcement of conventional morality, without its being internalized by a child, seems a consistent part of the pattern leading to authoritarian personalities. Concern for autonomy steadily attempts to counteract that merely legalistic, "external" kind of morality.

Religious Faith as Trust

Understood as a goal of the pastor's work with people, autonomy is a part of religious faith. It is the "courage to be," to accept the self and to engage in living. A second dimension of faith, and the one more commonly designated by the term, is an awareness of our God-relation. Naming this awareness as a goal implies a broader range of pastoral functioning than would stem from such a restricted definition of pastoral care as that of Thurneysen: "Pastoral care is a means of leading [the] individual to sermon and sacrament and thus to the Word of God, of incorporating him into the Christian community, and of preserving him in it" (Thurneysen, 1962, p. 32). We ourselves may find it hard to believe there can be much fulfilled meaning in life outside the church, with its sermon and sacrament and Christian community, but holding to that definition of our goal too easily imperils the helping process. It can subvert autonomy or turn a shared quest into one-way preaching. Firet comments:

Pastoral care is . . . an address to an equal. . . . Perhaps this person has lost her way; she is flooded by a sense of inadequacy. But pastoral care means that she is addressed in the language of respect and dignity. However undignified and worthless she seems, pastoral care is primarily an acknowledgment of her in her dignity. However irresponsibly he may have lived, pastoral care is an acknowledgment of him in his freedom and responsibility, an acknowledgment which must often assume the form of helping him regain acceptance and experience of that freedom and responsibility. (Firet, 1986, p. 267)

In the broader sense, and in this context, I mean by faith something akin to that undergirding assurance in life that Erik Erikson calls "basic trust." In Erikson's scheme, this is a particularly strong psychological need of the infant, but it is a continuing need throughout life. Religion provides ritual rehearsal of basic trust, and it gives it intelligible verbal substance.

Faith as trust is expressed innumerable times in Scripture, especially in Psalms. God is refuge, strength, shepherd, parent, fortress, protector, guardian. In spite of the pestilence, the enemies, the assaults of grief and slander, God is to be trusted. Jesus' life-style and his preaching of the kingdom reassure especially the outcasts and disinherited that God cares for them. They are worth much more than the sparrow and God takes account of even that sparrow's fall. Paul stresses the deliverance God works in Christ, so that nothing in the cosmos can separate us from God's caring love in Christ.

Engagement

A sense of self and trust in the God-relation issue into engagement with the world. Erikson asserts that other stages in the child's development, building on basic trust, include an outreach into the world. He writes of the need in school-age children to grow toward "initiative" and "industry" rather than fall back into their opposites, self-doubt, guilt, and inferiority. In the healthy adult, Erikson stresses the capacity for "intimacy" and "generativity," overcoming the less healthy forces of isolation, self-absorption, and stagnation (1959, pp. 50-100). For H. Richard Niebuhr, trust alone is not an adequate definition of faith's substance. He prefers love of God, and he incorporates this active element into it with the term *loyalty*. To love God means loyalty and love toward those God loves, and loyalty to God's causes (1956, p. 35).

It is this active element in faith that interests us especially, of course, as we think of the minister as moral counselor. Loyalty to God leads us to seek out a responsible moral pattern for our living.

The work of the moral counselor must be grounded in respect for the other and in the God-relation. Otherwise moral counsel can easily devolve into ineffective and imperious moralizing, or, on the part of the counselee, into a shallow, judgmental activism in the world.

Autonomy, trust, and engagement with the world are three dimensions of religious faith. Action in the world involves a discovery of vocation, a feeling for one's place in the story of God's involvement with the world. To know something of vocation is to be engaged as servant of God's cause in some way—as parent, friend, contemplative, activist, reformer, citizen, breadwinner, caregiver, courageous sufferer. Health of spirit involves a sense of belonging in the world for the world's good. It is the opposite of coming at life sensuously or exploitatively: "What can I get out of it?" The single-minded pursuit of private happiness, apart from the moral backdrop, is a dead-end pursuit.

Effective Help

The counselor with a moral vision is a therapist for the human soul. Lewis Andrews, a young psychologist who works primarily with drug abusers, has written about the growing movement away from "conventional" in favor of what he calls "ethical" therapy. For Andrews, the therapy involves far more than listening and empathy; it involves encouragement in structured living and active guidance or teaching from the therapist or therapy group.

Andrews reviews research that raises questions about the effectiveness of some psychotherapy. To illustrate, he cites among others a study at the Kaiser Foundation Hospital. One year there was such a flood of requests for counseling that twenty-three patients were put on a waiting list for six months. Staff psychologists hoped to demonstrate the worth of their program by using the twenty-three as a control, charting the progress of those in treatment and those deprived of it. As Andrews sums up, "To everyone's surprise, those who received no help in tranquilizing their anxieties, either through drugs or the assurance of regular counseling, improved at least as well as those in therapy."[1]

---

1. 1987, p. 133. The research is documented in M. Gross, *The Psychological Society* (New York: Random House, 1978).

On the other hand, Andrews cites, as does pastoral theologian Tom Oden in a similar vein (1974, p. 13), the effectiveness of the "Anonymous" groups. Lay-led, the groups offer procedures rather different from the kind of client-centered listening that is so basic in conventional counseling. They provide a community of moral energy and concern. Reformist goals for the individual are always there, as is methodical guidance, like the "Twelve Steps" of AA or Narcotics Anonymous. We have already cited AA as the best resource for helping alcoholics.

The trend toward a stronger theological and moral underpinning for pastoral counseling does not emerge from academic theological critique of our psychological preoccupations alone. It results from frustrations with the shallower goals and the limited success of much secular therapy. Important as the insights of the therapeutic period may have been, Oden's deeper question remains: After therapy what? What do we hope for, believe in, and do? These are religious and moral questions. The force field of our concerns does include our learnings from the client-centered approach. However, much as we learn from the psychological disciplines, the minister need not defer to psychotherapy as if it could provide answers for all the questions of method, purpose, and ultimate meanings in our work with people.

The Calling of the Pastor

Community mental health professionals identify the minister as one of the helping agents for people in mental and emotional difficulty. Indeed, some mental health professionals, relatively unacquainted with church and synagogue life, have expressed surprise at the extent of this pastoral care (Mollica et al., 1986; Gurin et al., 1960).

For three reasons at least, we have accepted this assessment of our work with some satisfaction. We have seen in our own pastoral experience that we have been helpful to people in distress. In a secularizing age, we have experienced enough professional malaise to be grateful for appreciation from mental health professionals. And the cultural forces of our "therapeutic age" have allowed us to affirm a mental health definition for the pastoral dimensions of our work to complement more traditional, more theological language for it.

We should view our own satisfaction at this point with some skepticism. Our fundamental calling, according to both social analysis and religious tradition, is something else. And according to our own religious self-definition, our work is not wholly continuous with the world of mental health, deeply grateful for the vast network of care and healing though we must be. Many of the saints have been psychological oddballs. Probing the discontinuity, Albert Schweitzer wrote a psychiatric study of Jesus.

From our point of view, in simple sociological terms a culture needs a symbol system of greater depth than one organized around the language of mental health, self-fulfillment as salvation, and therapist as priest. In the long run a larger statement of meanings is called for. Priest and cult have had a larger role than fostering adjustment and psychological equilibrium, desperately though they are needed by the mentally ill and the neurotic. The human hunger is for transcendent meaning, for peace with God. This meaning may create disequilibrium as well as balance. It brings prophetic criticism as well as pastoral assurance. It undergirds integrity and sparks the moral drive of the reformer. It makes us restless until we find our rest in God. A merely therapeutic model for faith-building pastoral care is inadequate.

The psychologist Paul Pruyser reports with dismay his experience at the Menninger Foundation, where he has been involved in clinical training for clergy. Pastors "sat at the feet of the psychiatric Gamaliels," without reciprocal offerings of theological perspective to the doctors and nurses. They "were eager to absorb as much psychological knowledge and skill as they could, without even thinking of instructional reciprocity." It was a "one-sided" dialogue (1976, pp. 23, 24). In assessing the problems of patients and parishioners, the pastors seemed to forget their own vocational gifts and resources, turning to a psychological terminology in place of pastoral and theological language. Pruyser boldly proposes some "diagnostic" variables from among theological categories, arguing that clergy are called and urgently needed for this kind of counsel with those who turn to them. It is not insignificant, says Pruyser, that people turn to the minister instead of the psychologist or psychiatrist. Whether conscious of it or not, they have a sense that their troubles are soul-size matters, begging some of the ultimate questions religious leaders are especially called to address.

Much as we have gained from the modern movements in pastoral counseling, we need to recognize how much they depart from the long tradition of guidance by the bishops, the priests, and the pastors over the centuries. John T. McNeill, introducing his important *History of the Cure of Souls* in 1951, wrote with this stress on the pastoral vocation:

Socrates was, and wished to be, *iatros tes psuches,* a healer of the soul. These Greek syllables have been recast to form the word "psychiatrist." But Socrates would hardly recognize the medical psychiatrist as a member of his fraternity. A scientific psychiatry indifferent to religion and philosophy is a new and strange phenomenon. Whatever may be the future importance of this new science, it is abundantly evident that the role of the religious physician of souls is not played out. . . . He stands in a long and honorable tradition . . . [and has] membership in a unique and sacred profession. (p. viii)

The pastor learns from the psychological disciplines, which may contribute to the mental health of a parishioner, but the vocation of ministry offers a different perspective, whether always complementary to that of the therapist or not.

Our discussion must now turn more explicitly to the processes of pastoral care and counsel, as illumined by this emphasis on the minister as moral counselor. The next chapter begins with a case study. Using it, we can outline some implications our perspective generates for the work of pastoral care.

CHAPTER FOUR

George F. and
the Process of Counsel

GEORGE F., AGED 32, IS MARRIED TO A COLLEGE
graduate; he himself had a half-year at a fundamentalist
Bible college and then completed a bachelor's degree at a
state college. George is a manufacturer's regional sales
representative; he and his wife have no children.

George presents himself to the pastor, a few weeks after
beginning to attend the church, and says he is suffering
from a problem of "always feeling rushed." He is always
trying to please other people, and yet at the same time, he
reports, he is usually overcritical of others. Again, he
"always" feels he has failed when he doesn't make a sale.

George reads a lot—Weatherhead, Peale, Peck, Billy
Graham. He criticizes his spouse for spending so much of
her time with television and murder mysteries and with
gossip and bridge. His neighbors think George is an oddball
for reading so much. His wife wonders where he is when he
is out, and he thinks she checks up on him.

George is open about his background. His father is stern,
overbearing, and has lost one leg below the knee, the result
of a war injury. His mother is "overly religious," a onetime
member of a Primitive Baptist group, presently more
mainline than that.

Invited to continue his story, George remembers that his
father and mother "had sexual relations" within sight of the

children when the children were quite small. His father always seemed to present himself as perfect; yet he saw the father once in a compromising situation with another woman. George also once learned that his father drank a lot as a young man.

At a second conference, George "reports progress." He attributes the gains to a shift into an office assignment, with more regular hours, and to his plans for buying a house in a stable section of the community. Soon, however, he is recounting specific instances of great frustration and anger. At a bridge party, someone criticized him for overbidding his hand; he left the table. He is emotionally riled because the men in his neighborhood talk of little but women and sex all the time. On a sales trip, he and a partner were offered the companionship of two "girls" after quitting work at nine in the evening. George declined, but his buddy went through with it, and in the process won both a sale and the friendship of a local dealer.

George makes something positive of a recent "satisfactory" episode in which his wife did not complain of his "uncooperativeness" when he stayed home for an evening while she went out to a neighbor's for talk. He feels he might now start joining some clubs to get something above the ordinary level of conversation with others. He says he has "depressions for short periods, when nothing prompts them," sometimes as short as twenty minutes.

George shares more of his background at this session as well. His mother's four brothers are or were all alcoholics; her three sisters and she are all "fine church women." George's own sister was married successfully, but lives far from home. His younger brother, 23, is a no-good who has had but six months of college work, at two different schools; he was married at age 18, but divorced within a year. There was a child, born in seven months, and "some people" said the baby was not his own. The wedding had taken place about two months after the boy's return from military service, which was when he had first met the girl. George called the girl a "tramp." The brother had sent fifty dollars a week for the child for a while, and then later, when the brother had "taken off," the family had kept up the payments. No one knew now the whereabouts of the brother. He had surfaced once in Georgia, and later in Philadelphia, at times when he needed money. He had been a big disappointment to the family; George is disgusted with him, and won't help again if asked. The family has now stopped sending money for the child.

At the third interview, George begins by saying everything is "fine." He feels himself really to be searching, and partially finding, "a new life." As the interview progresses, however, old problems come out again, mainly: (1) "feeling others are judging" him, and that he is "always trying to meet their approval," and (2) that he himself is still too judgmental toward others, as, for instance, when the neighborhood men talk about sex and he gets "tremendously angry." He has been reading *The Courage to Be* again, and still doubts God. Nonetheless, if there is a God, he thinks he has "measured up, O.K." Later in the conference, he tells the story of his wife's father, who was unfaithful to his wife for many years, so that now, when George sees him, he still cannot talk to him or "accept him as a regular person," even though George's wife and her brother "accept him fine." The pastor and George schedule a fourth interview, both feeling that they are making some headway, and that George, and possibly soon his wife, may come more regularly into the life of the church.

Pastoral Perspectives

The variables in what we do not know from such reports as this are infinite, of course. It matters whether the pastor is a man or a woman. It matters whether the counselor's nonverbal expressions of face and gesture intensify at moments of psychological, or religious, or moral interest. No counselor or therapist is wholly "neutral" in these respects. It matters whether George has been at worship or other activities of the church, and, if he has been, what the content and quality of these experiences were.

The pastor wants to be of help to George. But what is

"help" in George's mind, and what will help him most? That George approaches a minister instead of a counselor may come about because of accessibility and economics. However, it is better to assume that he sees his problems, at least subconsciously, to have religious implications as well as psychological ones. He is clearly open to conversation that uses religious language.

George is on a serious-minded pilgrimage, seeking help. His present anguish and his unattractive traits should not obscure for us the fact that he has struggled valiantly to overcome handicaps in his family of origin, handicaps he describes with some objectivity. He distinguishes himself from his alcoholic uncles, his overbearing father, his "overly religious" mother, his younger brother, his father-in-law. The energy in George's intentionality is impressive. One might say he tries too hard, but we would not do him justice to consider him simply a victim of determinative childhood forces into which he needs more insight. We have spoken (in chapter 2) of the inadequacy in a model of impairment or victimization compared to a more dynamic sense of human possibility.

A minister can respond to George with a psychological perspective on his problems, or a more theological viewpoint. The two need not necessarily conflict, but they inevitably lead to different nuances in the counseling relationship. They make for different responses and initiatives by the pastor. We can list a few of the differences around recurrent themes in this brief account from George and the pastor.

1. Initially George says he is always feeling rushed. He tries to please others. The pastor may think in psychological terms like this: George needs to learn to relax. He is too insecure. The sources of support and affection for him were woefully inadequate when he was a child. Or, more theologically, the reasoning may proceed like this: George has yet to trust God or some sustaining ground of his selfhood, his being. He is trying to justify himself, because he doesn't see the impossibility of that and doesn't know that in God's mercy it isn't necessary.

2. Again, George says he is "overcritical" of other people. In particular, he judges talk about "women and sex" by the neighborhood men (becoming possibly angry), and he can't accept his father-in-law as a "regular person" because of the latter's past extramarital affair. We may think about this judgmentalism as a lack of self-acceptance, a prudishness born of childhood sex-related trauma such as the exposed parental intercourse, or an instance of overly critical superego. Or we can again put it in broader terms, in a perspective which, in light of the pastor-parishioner setting, is appropriate: George may need to work through an understanding of sexuality as a good part of God's creation, problematic as sex seems to be for him. Moreover, George fails to intuit the world as communal. He moralistically distances himself from others. To use traditional language, he does not think of himself and others as redeemed sinners. He does not sense that, in spite of all the tawdriness and meanness of the race, we are created for one another in a common humanity and called to common service.

3. George reads a lot. We can view the reading as an escape, an ambitious self-improvement campaign, a source of pride, or as a quest born of the heart's restlessness. The counselor will listen to find out more, but the counselor's understanding of human nature and aspiration affect the listening. For George, the reading is probably a little of each. The pastor hopes to deepen George's understanding of his own behavior without necessarily changing his behavior at all.

4. With George we can rehearse a psychological past, or think more about his vocation as human and as believer. We can aim directly at helping him achieve for himself a better measure of self-esteem, or we can allow a stronger self to emerge along with a maturing of his Christian faith.

Moral Reflections

Moral dimensions of the pastor's work with George emerge along the way. Fundamentally, there is the choice to engage George as parishioner rather than patient, to relate to him as a person with problems he is working on, rather than as a victim of a problematic history, a patient we intend to heal. This is not to deny the power of the unconscious in shaping George's behavior. George knows about this power. He reports the bridge-party rage and the depressions as times when he felt overcome by internal forces. But we are not insight therapists. Our attitude, along with George's, will shape the conversation toward an assumption that this is a struggle George is undertaking, a struggle for deeper faithfulness and a more settled, patient peace of soul.

In regard to the accounting George makes of himself, there are explicit aspects of his moral attitude and moral choices that can be discussed in the interviews, if they continue. Such discussions will integrate George's experience of life into a broader world view, or faith view, than would a purely psychological discourse about George's feelings. In this brief case study, there are at least six avenues open for shared reflection and moral growth.

1. George criticizes his wife's use of her time. There is a moral issue involved in the judgments George aims at his wife. George criticizes her for reading murder mysteries, while reading a lot himself. There is a moral issue involved in attending to the tasks of companionship in marriage and to affirming a spouse in her own self-expression. Judging by George's self-awareness, he and the pastor can discuss both these matters—the judging of others about their choices for leisure time, and the building up of a marriage. Quite probably, were George's wife open to it, marriage counseling would be helpful to the two of them. George did not ask for that, however; he knows more is at stake.

2. George reports openly on the past. His moralism prevents him from accepting his father without strenuous, destructive resentment. In light of the imperfections and injuries that constitute a large part of the past, for George to ground himself in a sense of a gracious Providence is no small task in Christian faith. A struggle toward such maturity in faith, however, is more likely to offer George a way forward than extended complaints about the past. At this point the pastor will distinguish between moralism and

the moral maturity that can accept, forgive, and let go the past.

3. George reports a loss of self-control in moments of anger, citing in particular a time when he was criticized. Here our psychological competence is undoubtedly called on. George needs insight into the genesis of such powerful emotions. Yet, this too is a moral matter. George must be allowed to confess his failures as such. Insight will lead to less of a sense of helplessness, of victimization by these surges of emotion. But it would be counterproductive to explain them away as the result of the emotional condition. They are also part of the human condition for which we take responsibility in the God-relation, which we confess, and for which we are forgiven. George may want to take conciliatory steps in interpersonal relationships to heal broken ties with his friends. We respect him in his efforts to be more patient and we allow him to use us as a symbol of a better way for dealing with criticism.

The deeper alienation from others, evident in George's comments about his younger brother and his father-in-law, invites further discussion. Reconciliation on a relatively easy plane—with the people at the bridge party, for example— may foster conversation about the more painful instances of broken community.

4. George complains about the sales partner who took advantage of the nighttime offer of casual sex *and* who made the sale. "Why do the wicked prosper?" In pastoral conversation, George would be helped by reflection on the costs of being loyal to his own standards. Does he hold expectations of reward for being good? Is his morality simply a more sophisticated or more religious kind of self-seeking? George's comment about "having measured up" give strong evidence that his faith at this point is woefully underdeveloped.

5. The "fine church women" bears exploring. Is there any sarcasm in the comment? If not, George's positive feelings about the church are an important asset. Conversation about the nature of the community of faith, and about the redemptive, community-building message of its

Scriptures, is in order. Psychologically, the church represents a source of healing for George's isolation. Morally and spiritually, it can provide an environment for growth in faith that addresses the issues named above.

The Process of Counsel

Given a heightened consciousness of its moral dimension, we must now describe more generally the process of counsel.

1. With Linda Philby or George F., as with any other parishioner, the pastor begins by listening. This is "active listening" that demonstrates the concern, the "positive regard," the affirmation we hold out for the parishioner. It is inevitably conditioned by the listener's interests and world view, but in the first instance, it must be as open as possible. It is all too easy to divert the parishioner from the central concerns that may have prompted the pastoral visit. Those concerns may be some time in surfacing, and we must introduce no distractions during that period.

Our goal at this point is twofold. First, it is to establish rapport with the parishioner, to build trust. The first problem being presented is often a safer subject for discussion, used to test whether the level of trust warrants deeper self-disclosure. We want to show that we care and can be trusted. Second, it is our goal to understand, as accurately and sensitively as we are able, the parishioner's sense of his or her situation. We want to avoid twisting the parishioner's report to fit an ideological mold of our own about the nature of the human condition. We also want to comprehend, beneath that sense, the unspoken feelings and attitudes and beliefs about the world.

As "moral counselors," we listen for spoken and unspoken commitments. What are the structures and loyalties that condition, limit, and direct the person's choices? Linda is struggling with issues of commitment and her own happiness, even as she inquires about a pastor's opinion. George has stepped free of his family of origin, seeking a life for himself and his wife. In following his account, however, it becomes clear that he is still deeply enmeshed in family relationships, and that growth in religious faith is a subtle part of his struggle.

The assumption of Rogerian counseling, the most influential model for today's pastors, is that within most troubled persons there are resources for a better life and for problem-solving, given the empathy of a good counselor and the clarification that can come with counsel. This assumption is congruent with the first of our goals as pastoral caregivers, autonomy. The pastor does not give Linda an answer that would make her dependent, or childish. It is her life, her decision. The pastor does not take over the conversation with George, turning it into an interrogation until at some key moment a prescription is offered.

2. Much of our pastoral care is adequately carried forward on the principles of Rogerian counseling. However, another set of options, allowing a larger and more distinctive kind of pastoral initiative, must now be suggested. These options can only be exercised once rapport is well established. Counseling is a gentle art. Reviewing a verbatim report from an usually moving counseling session, William Oglesby writes:

There is a mystery in the emergence of faith. It cannot be programmed, nor can it be forced. At one and the same time it "happens," and the person participates in the "happening." . . . It is in no sense a decision in the ordinary meaning of that term although it becomes the basis for decisions of all sorts. It is for this reason that an appeal of the will is doomed to failure even though the person may engage in some sort of volitional activity.

(1980, pp. 107-8)

These options then are pathways for pastoral conversation that relates to the whole self of the parishioner, not merely to the thinking or the volition. "An appeal to the will is doomed to failure." As Oglesby goes on, citing Romans 7, "The will is in bondage." It needs more than exhortation. It is helpful to envision these as options that grow more and more available and even desirable over time, as the depth of relationship increases.

a. God-talk. One option is to introduce religious concepts, whether or not we use traditional or biblical language. This step will almost always evolve from and build on words and insights introduced by the parishioner. The counselee makes a passing reference to the sense of fulfillment in a job. The minister says: "It really seemed right that you were in that place; you felt almost called to be there." "Yes," responds the counselee, "I really did. And what's more . . ."

A parishioner reports feelings of bitterness toward another person, wishing he could shake it off. The pastor says, "It feels terribly hard to forgive something like that." And the conversation goes on, enriched and deepened with the quiet allusion to religious principle. That kind of initiative is inappropriate at first, but becomes increasingly appropriate as trust is built.

b. Self-disclosure. In professional counseling and psychotherapy, the counselor is guarded in self-disclosure. The focus is on the client's problems, and on his or her abilities to cope. From the start, the relationships of pastoral care are different. In other activities of parish life, the minister has disclosed his or her own personal perspectives and experiences in informal conversation, in small group life, in teaching, and in preaching. Stepping into counseling, we have to avoid deflecting a parishioner's self-report by more teaching or preaching. However, even with nonparishioners who come for counsel, over time in *pastoral* counseling the parson becomes a person rather than remain an anonymous "professional." That is a structural expectation in pastoral relationship. We share a common humanity with the parishioner, standing as we both do before God, in the presence of the Spirit. Each may testify to the other in terms of religious experience; each may learn from the other. The minister's moral convictions enter the conversation most easily as part of this self-disclosure, rather than as pronouncements about right and wrong.

c. Confrontation. A third option is confrontation. Again, this is a step that can succeed only within a relationship of trust. Confrontation is not a hostile step. It usually takes the form of an observation. "I notice that for the last half hour we have avoided any talk about parental responsibility in this relationship" (or honesty, or support, or affection). "You seem to me to become more troubled or hesitant when you talk about the profit you made in selling. Is that a polite reticence about money, or a feeling that you may have charged too much?"

A simple change of a name for something that has just been described often serves. A college professor was listening to a foreign student praise this country's openness in its immigration policy. The student then asserted that his own country's people would not allow that, because it would go against their cultural grain. "How do you feel about that racism yourself?" asked the instructor. A married man may describe his affair with another woman, without apparent moral concerns; given a strong rapport, it may be helpful if the counselor chooses the word *adultery* instead of the counselee's weaker word *affair.* Or a single young adult may describe a liaison in which his partner expects more than he will commit; the pastor can consider introducing the word *exploitation,* in a response that refers to the same relationship.

Introducing a new perspective into pastoral conversation cannot always build on the parishioner's own expression, of course. The time may come when the minister risks injecting an altogether new element into the dialogue. The pastor may take the step to avoid compromising his or her own integrity, so as not to be misunderstood. The minister may want to challenge the parishioner toward a new stage of growth, or want to prevent injury to another party. "In spite of what you are deciding, John, I want you to know that the tradition of the church takes an opposite point of view." "It seems to me that you are floating along enjoying life at a time when you could do a great deal more for others—and maybe in the process find a deeper kind of satisfaction." "No matter how great that solution would seem to you, I don't think it is in the best interest of those two children."

Confrontation is often necessary to maintain the same affirmation of the parishioner's selfhood that mandates serious listening at the beginning of a counseling relationship. That is to say, it is a sign of respect. Always to avoid disagreement, always to avoid leveling with a parishioner, is to demean that person, to treat him or her as a child, as less than an equal, less than a fellow human. It is to allow a false relationship to grow. "Respect," writes Ralph Underwood, "is a moral connection that discloses how empathy and certain ways of being confrontive require each other" (1985, p. 90).

d. Spiritual Direction. Although strictly speaking it is an option outside the counseling discipline, spiritual direction is an important part of ministry. The term immediately implies a stronger pastoral initiative than does a counseling model of pastoral care. While the therapist asks "What was your experience in childhood?" and the pastoral counselor asks "How are you getting on now with your spouse?" the spiritual director asks, "What is your relation to God?" That is, the therapist tends to focus on intrapsychic dynamics, the counselor more on interpersonal tension, and the director on the experience of God in prayer. One can easily see the significance of moral counsel for spiritual direction. God is often encountered as moral claim. Remembering this perspective, we may invite reflection on our relation to God as creative guide and lawgiver, instead of simply as forgiving divine parent.

Kenneth Leech calls the director "spiritual friend." Friends can take creative liberties in their conversation, initiatives that are not strictly "client-centered." They can enter robust controversy that leads on to probing moral reflection.

e. Scripture. The Bible, of course, is the book of the faith, and it plays a fundamental role in our moral perspectives. A larger section—the following chapter—is warranted for treating the nature of scriptural authority in moral counsel.

CHAPTER FIVE

Using, Not Abusing, the Bible

As far as we can tell, our pastor did not quote the Bible to George F. "Judge not," he might have said, because of the holier-than-thou moralism that was part of George's alienation from members of his own family and of friction with his wife. The pastor might have reassured George with one of the Ten Commandments: "You did well on your sales trip. After all, 'Thou shalt not commit adultery.' " Mark Jones could have told Linda, "Well, the Bible says, . . ." and quote one of the biblical positions on divorce. Moral counsel avoids using the Bible in so simplistic a way for good reason.

The Bible is the indispensable source book for Christian faith. It is Scripture, with all that Scripture means for a religious tradition. We refer to it as the written Word of God, and the primary task of ordained ministry is often simply defined as proclamation of the Word. The pastor, says Jacob Firet, "mediates the coming of God in his Word" (1986, p. 14). Eduard Thurneysen even sums up the whole purpose of pastoral care as proclamation. Karl Barth says the Christian vocation is to witness to the Word.

Clearly, Christians mean something more by the Word than the canonical written books of the Bible. The Word is God's dynamic power for the believer's wholeness, embodied in more than the written words. In the Fourth Gospel, Christ is called the word, the *logos,* enfleshed in human form. Just as clearly, however, the written Bible holds an authoritative place for the Christian community. But the Bible can be both used and abused in the minister's role as moral counselor.

Moral injunctions pervade the Bible. The Pentateuch provides long sections of detailed guidance not only about procedures for Israelite feast days but also about caring for the poor, greeting the stranger, honesty with one's compatriots, marital fidelity. Proverbs, part of the Wisdom literature, is an extended collection of aphorisms, many of them moral in nature, like the sayings of Ben Franklin's Poor Richard. The gospel record of Jesus' teachings is not all parables. The so-called Q source provides many moral sayings. And the epistles, Pauline and pastoral, rehearse moral instructions of both general and particular import, from "Bless those who persecute you" (Rom. 12:14*a*), to "Let deacons be married only once" (I Tim. 3:12*a*). The Bible, indeed, has been called a rule book for the Christian life; given its authoritative role for the faith community, one would easily think that Scripture offers a coherent code for the people of God.

The role of Scripture, however, is far more subtle than the straightforward provision of a code. To think of it as a rulebook, and to quote from it on that assumption, leads easily to abuse of the Bible, often as we do it. In actuality, such citations imply less (or more) than that simplistic assumption, as we shall see.

Pastors and lay people can be forgiven considerable confusion over how to use the Bible these days.[1] As but one example, we can reflect on the raging debates over homosexuality. Serious-minded authorities to whom we have customarily deferred—seminary theologians, denominational study groups and legislative assemblies, religiously oriented social scientists—while strenuously disagreeing with

---

1. The following material is taken from my article in the *Christian Century* of April 4, 1979, "How Shall We Use the Bible Now?" Copyright 1979 Christian Century Foundation. Reprinted by permission.

one another, all suggest biblical warrants, in letter or in spirit, for their arguments.

Old questions come at us in new ways. In what sense can the Bible be called authoritative when a whole battery of critical tools shows us the ways in which it is culturally and historically conditioned by its time? In what sense may we argue that "the Bible says" anything, now that we know the multiplicity of its traditions and moral perspectives, its authors, and its literary genres? And the broader questions remain as well: Why go to the Bible, this particular set of books, to the exclusion, say, of the Gospel of Thomas from Nag Hammadi or of the classics of Christian literature? What difference does it make that something was said and written 2,000 years ago? How do we give it authority and translate it into something significant and appropriate for guidance in the very different modern world? We must look first at the nature of biblical authority before dealing with it as a sourcebook for moral counsel. If the authority question were a simple matter, we would come closer to having an agreed-on ethic, polity, life-style, and gospel in the churches, all less variegated according to class and culture.

The Question of Authority

Leaving parish pastors to one side for a moment, there is hardly a consensus about the ways academic theologians themselves defer to Scripture. That is the conclusion of David Kelsey as he analyzes the uses of Scripture in recent theology. For one theologian, doctrinal propositions themselves, once dug out of Scripture, are authoritative. For another, the events or the persons behind the narratives represent the locus of revelation. For yet another, center stage is taken by the existential insight prompted when a person or a Christian community truly encounters the Bible story.

Part of the difficulty in reading out of Scripture a common guidance for Christians is the log in our own eyes, more technically, of course, "the hermeneutic circle." We cannot help coming to Scripture with cultural conditioning of some sort. David Lochhead writes about what might be called the ideological captivity of our hermeneutic—the fact that we focus on one aspect of Scripture or another from the outset. Reading Exodus, for example, a Western liberal may emphasize the evolution of a higher monotheism in Israel. The Third World Christian may stress the liberating implications of Israel's escape from Egyptian bondage. And a conservative may stress the gracious and stabilizing gift of the law at Sinai. Any argument that this part of the Bible offers a single message for the people of God vanishes. What then happens to biblical authority? What happens to our frequent assertions that the text "says" this or that?

James Barr puts the questions another way. He asks "whether the whole subject of 'authority' should be continued, or whether an entirely different organization of the matter has to be considered" (1973, p. 113). Consider only the issue of what it is about the Bible to which we want to ascribe normative importance. Is it the intention of a biblical writer we are trying to get at, or the revelatory events to which the writer is responding, or, leaving all that aside, the literary material as it is, with its narrative and mythic power for the reader?

If authority is no longer the most helpful concept, just what will describe the way we approach the Bible and use it in moral counsel? It now seems useful to focus on the Bible's function rather than on its innate authority. This approach offers us a refreshing honesty. Without question, the Bible serves crucial functions in the life of the church, even if for the present we play down its formal "authority" because that is such an ambiguous category.

1. The Bible serves as the language of the church. It provides the church community its primary common source of imagery, allusion, and vocabulary. Our human outlook and thought processes are not only creatively shaped but also defined by the tools at our disposal in the very language we use. Without a rich vocabulary, our thinking is shallow, lacking nuance. In this sense, the Bible, even variously interpreted, helps hold the *oikumene* together and exerts considerable "authority." The better we know the wealth of story and religious expression in the Bible, the richer will be our life as a Christian community.

Part of this language-providing function of the Bible is community-building. We are, as James Gustafson calls us (1961), a "community of language"—analogous, for example, to an English-speaking community amid a Portuguese or Turkish culture. The church that is forever seeking out a newfangled idiom for expressing the faith and proclaiming the gospel at the expense of, rather than as a complement to, regular usage of biblical imagery is likely to find itself drying up as a community of Christians in touch with, and drawing strength from, the broader church. Even a socially radical congregation, on the other hand, while living in tension with the conservative environment of other churches, will, if it claims biblical language as its own, be less likely to lose its ability to witness in their midst.

Biblical language, because it is already the background of so much of Christian life, will say more than we mean it to say. It will evoke memory and reflection and nuanced meaning far beyond a use of secular "equivalents."

The Bible, understood as language for the church, exerts its authority indirectly. Decisions for church order and church action derive from the church community, nourished and shaped by biblical language and world view. Its leaders may rationalize and defend church policy and teaching by citing biblical norms, as if reading directly from a set of instructions. But their reading is necessarily selective. It is interpretive. Biblical authority is indirect.

It is the same for personal Christian morality. Our decisions about which biblical injunctions to cite, and which to put aside are partly functions of our culture, our own autonomous reasoning, and our religious experience. We are not passive in our perception of Scripture. (Do we stone the one who gathers sticks on the sabbath [Num. 15:35-36]? Do we follow the *lex talionis*, an eye for an eye [Exod. 21:24]? Do we urge persons in slavery to "regard their masters as worthy of all honor" [I Tim. 6:1])? We interpret one part of the Bible in terms of the whole, and that in light of our own time. Rather than a codebook, Scripture for us is most importantly a source of language and imagery. That is how it nurtures in us a conscientious mindset and generous disposition toward the human neighbor and the world.

2. Another function of the Bible is symbolic: It represents for us a "voice from outside." It reminds us that we, one generation and the next, are not concocting religion *de novo,* and that we do not save ourselves. Comprehending this symbolic function helps us understand those who still prefer, for example, Paul in the King James Version. Nostalgia and familiarity are part of their sentiment, to be sure. But these people know that clarity is not the major factor in the choice of a text. The morning lessons are not so much thoughts for the day as parts of our liturgical action. "Hear the word of God," we say, and we read an ancient piece of prose or poetry, somewhat obscure for most of the listeners, and often contradicted in historical detail or even theological posture by some other portion of Scripture, at least on the surface. All this is not so much a direct citation of literal authority as an evocative step in worship.

One aspect of this symbolic function of the Bible is its role as a book of devotion. Most of the Bible was designed otherwise than as a text for private meditation. It was a collective memory bank, and a resource for corporate use in the cultus. It included letters addressed to particular problems at Corinth and Philippi, and hero legends from a bygone age. Yet the Bible has had a profound influence through its devotional use, not merely because it offers so much insight in its substance, but because it is the Christian's holy book. The evocative power of the daily texts cited in books of devotion is increased tenfold by attribution because they come from the Bible.

3. Not only is Scripture our language and our symbol for transcendence, but it is also story and parable in our midst. A good story does not impose one-dimensional meaning on its reader. It invites response, evokes surprise, self-knowledge, reflection, commitment. It challenges not only our rational faculties but the imagination as well. In the case of religious story, it is more likely to provoke an encounter of the whole self with the divine—rather than of merely the

rational part of us alone. Biblical theology is "recital," wrote
the distinguished Old Testament scholar G. Ernest Wright.

We do not read a good story and afterward reduce its
import to a proposition, thus rendering the story unnecessary. We may even ask that the story be repeated, for the
sheer experience of hearing it again, not to get a better
chance for deciphering it. The great modern dance artist
Martha Graham, asked what a dance of hers meant, is
reported to have said, "Darling, if I could tell you, I would
not have danced it."

The Moral Use of the Bible

The foregoing discussion prepares us for a more direct
discussion of the Bible's role vis-à-vis the minister's work as
moral counselor.

1. First, it is clear that the Bible is not most basically a
rulebook. Its fundamental gift is not that of an imperious
law laid upon willing or unwilling subjects, but the gift of
wholeness that comes from knowing a gracious God. The
Bible tells a story of a people, old and new Israel. That story
forms us into a Christian community, and it nurtures us in
our identity. In that community, we are shaped and
sustained in Christian character. As the graciousness of God
is rehearsed and celebrated in that community, we are
invited, in our freedom, to respond appropriately. Our root
dispositions and intentions are nudged and liberated
toward altruism. Our defensiveness is lessened, given the
sustaining care of God. Morally speaking, the church is first
a "community of character" (Hauerwas) before it is a
community of moral discourse and moral discipline. Those
two follow after: We reflect on the Word and establish rules
and guidelines for the sake of Christian witness and service.

2. The Bible provides us language for the moral
enterprise. This "language" is far more basic than a
vocabulary for ethical reasoning in face of new occasions
that provoke new duties. It is the imagery of story more than
the content of precept. We do not literally copy the life of
Moses or Hannah or Amos, of Jesus or Mary or Paul as we

go about our discipleship. Their stories, however, are in the back of our minds as we ponder the moral questions of our day and as we shape our lives toward faithfulness—Moses' leadership toward liberation and his gift of torah, Hannah's trust and hope, Amos' prophetic courage in denouncing moral corruption, Jesus' self-sacrifice, Mary's grief, Paul's indefatigable witness.

Christian morality arises from conversion more than coercion. Jean Piaget, whose pioneering work, *The Moral Judgment of the Child* is cited later, sees two kinds of morality in children. He finds a morality of duty in the younger child, a morality of constraint born of parental proscription and prescription. This is gradually replaced by a morality of cooperation. The first is "heteronomous," coming from outside the young child, for whom the right is whatever the adult says is right; the latter is autonomous, springing from a maturing sense of fairness and equity, from an ability to identify with other persons. Christian morality is more like the latter than like the former. "After those days," writes Jeremiah, speaking for Jahweh, "I will put my law within them, and I will write it upon their hearts. . . . No longer shall each [one] teach [the] neighbor . . . saying, 'Know the Lord,' for they shall all know me, from the least of them to the greatest" (31:33, 34).

All this does not, of course, solve the paradox of law and gospel. The paradigm at the heart of the Christian story is the Christ who empties himself to become a slave, the one who lays down his life that others might live abundantly. That kind of agape does not come from legislation; it comes from trust and loyalty to God and the good. The Christian community arrives at its codes and its decisions about the moral good within a consciousness nurtured by the Bible, but its actions reflect far more than simply the direct moral precepts and admonitions in the Bible. It speaks with the whole imagery of the biblical story as its formative language, and it inevitably speaks as well from within its own cultural milieu, from its own experience and its own communal reasoning.

3. Third, the Bible mediates an apprehension of transcendence. Through it we are in touch with that crucible

time in history from which we take our origins. Call it Israel-event, call it Christ-event, call it Revelation. Without reducing it to a set of petty rules, or even to a neat package of moral principles, the Bible represents for us the Moral Law, the truth that rightness and wrongness are rooted in God's will. The Bible symbolizes for us the objectivity of the moral. Sheer relativism is answered by the patriarch's "Hear O Israel," by the prophet's "Thus says the Lord," and by Jesus' "I say unto you." For the believer, these affirmations point to what Martin Luther King meant when he said that the arc of the universe bends toward justice.

Pastors are charged with the responsibility of helping whole congregations of people ground their lives in that confidence. They are not to exploit the numinous for their own gain or for manipulating parishioners into thinking in the pastor's mold, their moral systems cloned from the pastor's. They are not to tame the holy by domesticating its moral demands until the membership think they live up to the whole of the law. They are to point toward the holy, toward God's justice and God's mercy, so that the moral life can proceed, rooted and grounded in faith.

Supremely, of course, this happens in good preaching. Scholars have taken note of the present-day divergence of biblical studies and Christian ethics (Birch and Rasmussen, 1976). The Bible doesn't make today's ethical decisions for us. But the great moral weight of the scriptural tradition cannot be avoided in responsible preaching—the care for the poor and the outcast, faithfulness and forgiveness in human relations to echo God's own, the fruits of the spirit, the Golden Rule. The Bible points to the transcendent grounding of the moral life.

There are appropriate times in pastoral care for using the Bible as a pointer toward the transcendent. A parishioner, in the throes of a moral dilemma, may seek strength to take the harder course, the costly one, the less ego-centered one. Pastoral conversation may point to Jesus as the model *par excellence,* and to his teachings, which are congruent with his life: "Give to [the one] who begs from you" (Matt. 5:42). "Love your enemies" (Matt. 5:44). "Take up [your] cross and follow me" (Matt. 16:24). A parishioner may fear risks involved in what is perceived to be the right direction. The promise that God accompanies us into the future is morally affirming. In relation to a confession of a grievous wrong, or to a person's sense of having violated divine law, the Bible can bring a knowledge of forgiveness. One thinks of Psalms (103, 130) and of Jesus' various encounters with sinners and with those in need of healing. Reconciling the person to God and to the neighbor is one more role of being moral counselor.

Biblical Precept and Admonition

What then is the status of biblical laws and moral precepts? We know them to be culturally conditioned, and often at odds with one another. ("You have heard," says Jesus often, "but I say." To one he says "Give all you have to the poor," and to Zacchaeus, who gives but half, he says "Salvation has come to this house" [Luke 19:9].) Ancient ritual regulations and first-century household practices are mixed in with the Beatitudes and such perennial maxims as the Golden Rule. But at base, and this bears reiterating, the gift of God through Scripture is not a set of ethical rules. It is simply the Good News of God's grace and the promise of God's realm.

Biblical law and moral precept therefore serve as signs and celebrations of God's way with us as much as they serve as rules of life. I can preach from a text, a commandment from the decalogue, for example, but its power comes as scriptural symbol of God's transcendence as much as from its prescriptions. "Graven image" speaks of idolatry; it has a broader application than to stone and brass idols, and millions of my fellow Christians find in this commandment nothing to forbid their inspiring religious icons in worship. Honoring father and mother does not solve the dilemmas of placing them in a nursing home or supplementary Social Security payments for the indigent. "Do not steal" does not provide the Christian community details about fair return and unjust exploitation in the profits a transnational corporation takes out of a have-not nation.

The preachers and teachers of the church need to acknowledge that much more than a direct read-out of ancient texts is inevitable as the church uses the Bible. The texts summarize the law, the faithful path; they do not suggest the details of current moral life. They celebrate God's way with the human race and invite us to respond in kind. They are signs of the coming realm of God. But they do not of themselves adequately instruct me in what to do tomorrow at two in the afternoon. That grows from my own autonomy, nurtured by the Bible's story and my appropriation of it in my own particular Christian community. You and I are in dialogue with others through our mutual use of the Bible, but we do not, obviously, always come out at the same place.

What about George F.? If I am his pastor, I can legitimately use Scripture to underline his own idealism. If George suggests that he is being judgmental toward others, it is more appropriate to quote Matthew 7:1 ("Judge not") than a secular maxim ("People who live in glass houses shouldn't throw stones"). If a discussion focuses on the pride of church people and the heartiness of some who are not in the church, a reference to the parable of the Pharisee and the publican or to the elder brother (of Luke 15) may help move the discussion forward. If George moves toward a softer attitude about his younger brother, the one who has not been heard from, his own emerging compassion may be reinforced by alluding to the occasion when Peter asked about forgiveness and heard "not seven times, but seventy times seven." But these are to be seen as symbolic steps offered in support of a growing moral mindset. They will not be effective as injunctions imposed by the pastor. Our goal is autonomy, not regression into Piaget's "morality of constraint" for pre-adolescent children.

Many, many of the Bible's laws, from the decalogue to the Sermon on the Mount, are so consistent with the general moral thrust implicit in the Good News of God that we will cite them over and over. We will use them to summarize perspectives that we cherish and to symbolize God's justice and our fealty. We use them wrongly, however, if we imply that the faith is a code of conduct rather than a life-giving and liberating gift of God. In responding to that gift, we discover a moral task of large proportion indeed. We fail at it repeatedly, and must throw ourselves again upon God's mercy. The Word comes, and we move on again, both liberated and guided by it.

With all its internal diversity and historical conditioning, the Bible will exercise its "authority" with us in its own way. Misused by rigid human institutions and by proof-texting demagogues, it nonetheless nurtures and moves us in the faithful community if we have ears to hear. Let it be our language, the source of our imagery. Let it remind us that we do not author our own being or the truth of justice and love, but that God does. Let it speak the story from faith to faith, and evoke in us a love of the good, the beautiful. Its own authority, multifaceted and wholesome, can keep our hearts and minds centered on God. David Kelsey, discussing Karl Barth, puts it well:

The texts are authoritative not in virtue of any inherent property they may have, such as being inerrant or inspired, but in virtue of a function they fill in the life of the Christian community. To say that Scripture is "inspired" is to say that God has promised that sometimes, at his gracious pleasure, the ordinary human words of the Biblical texts will become the Word of God, the occasion for rendering an agent present to us in a Divine-human encounter.
(Kelsey, 1975, p. 47)

CHAPTER SIX

The Church,
the Pastor, and
Moral Education

NICK AND LINDA PHILBY'S TWO CHILDREN ARE considerably more active at St. Andrew's than their parents. The Philbys drop off their children at church and go back home as often as they stay for study and worship. Their own two careers make Sunday mornings precious for more than church going, and those other things, says Nick Philby, are also pretty important for the family's morale.

Mark, the pastor, wonders about the education St. Andrew's is offering those two Philby children and scores of others. It isn't that values are never mentioned. Every time Mark's assistant does the "children's moment" in the service, it seems to be a nice moralistic story. The adults eat it up. "That was sweet today, Harris," they say, or, "Just what we need to be telling the kids these days." But the children seem bored out of their Sunday frocks.

The goals statement of the Christian education program reassures Mark very little. It was drawn up by a lay committee after a curriculum discussion just before Mark's arrival at St. Andrew's. The statement seemed to focus on making the children both before and after confirmation into decent Christian citizens. They were to possess all the virtues promoted in the parish's Boy Scout troop with their "trustworthy, loyal, brave" ideals.

Mark has nothing much against the Boy Scouts. He is pleased that there is a troop at St. Andrew's, and he is proud of the lay members on the Troop Committee who take so much time with the boys on their outings. But Mark wants even more for kids than trustworthy, loyal, brave. He feels the need for a philosophy of moral education for the church school children that is deeper than rules of proper conduct.

Part of his concern, then, is theological. He and Harris have a set of teachers who mean very well. The teachers invest hours of time in preparing their lessons. But they need more guidance from Mark than he is yet able to give them, at least in respect to the nature of Christian perspectives on the moral life.

Another part of Mark's concern is pedagogical. Mark is struggling to become a better teacher himself, and he's not sure enough about how kids really learn, how they absorb ideas and attitudes and take them to heart. He sees them so often resembling a recalcitrant Old Testament Israel (just as some of their parents do). They "hear and hear, but do not understand" (Isa. 6:9).

Yet another part is simply pastoral. Mark is aware of the tension the two Philby children must experience in their home. He knows many others where it is worse, and he knows something of the struggles in the quarter of his congregation's children who live in single-parent families. Mark would like to bring the church school teachers in on his thinking. He would like the junior choir leader to think more deeply about her influence on Cheryl and Danny Philby and their friends. He is sure that the redemptive community should be doing even more for them than preaching the values of good citizenship.

The Dilemmas of Moral Education

Moral education in the church shares considerable common ground with the moral dimensions in pastoral care, discussed already. The autonomy and moral integrity of the individual and a spirit dedicated to service are ultimate goals of our teaching, rather than unreflective conformity to conventional norms. The temptations are similar: thinking that legislated rules of conduct will result in moral persons, thinking that telling is the same as teaching. Both faith and moral disposition toward the neighbor are more "caught" from experience than learned by verbal rote.

There is a difference to be noted, however, between the counseling of adults and the education of children. We can converse with adults on an equal footing, but with children we not only listen and evoke reflection, we also instruct. Disagreement about the scope of that difference lies behind many of the various debates that rage in education today.

The small child is egocentric, and our moral goal is altruism. Over time, those who begin as dependent, untutored children, extremely limited in reflective capacity, grow toward autonomy. The nature of that growth and the work of nurturing it are the substance of this heated controversy.

This debate may be illustrated by the thinking of two men who have written on moral education, Sidney Simon and Lawrence Kohlberg. They discuss a broad philosophy of education rather than exploring the specific concerns of a religious community, but their perspectives are relevant to the church.

During the 1960s, within the world of public education, Sidney Simon launched an educational movement around what he called "values clarification." Values clarification was helpful to many teachers for several reasons. It helped them define values clearly, distinguishing them from the facts of math or geography, yet legitimating their introduction into the public school curriculum. It offered explicit methods for moral education. And it seemed to avoid the problems of "indoctrination," a word that has come to refer to closed minds and a kind of partisan teaching that is inconsistent with education in a pluralistic society. Simon defined a value with several criteria. A value, he said, is something that we choose freely, from among alternatives, after thoughtful consideration; it is something that we cherish and publicly affirm, repeatedly; and it is a conviction we act on. Using such a definition, Simon argued that children in the grades and onward can learn to discuss values with one another and with their teachers. Although Simon and his colleagues worked in public education, church educators and youth group leaders added values clarification to their resources, some with great enthusiasm.

The advocates of values clarification hope to strengthen a child's appreciation of values without indoctrination. They assume that family and peers and the broader culture introduce and nurture ethical points of view, and that specific ethical teaching by the teacher is unnecessary and unadvisable. "If a child says he likes something, it does not seem appropriate for an older person to say 'You shouldn't like that,' " write Simon and several collaborators in one of the values clarification books (1966, p. 36). They continue:

Why must teachers see their role only as putting things into the mind of a child? . . . Why can't teachers learn to spend some of their time helping [a child] understand what the bewildering array of beliefs and attitudes that saturate our modern life are all about and which suits [the child] best? Is this not the road to values, to *clear* and *personal* values?

Gilbert Meilaender, a theologian, takes the assumptions of values clarification to task. "What an extraordinarily optimistic view of human nature is presupposed by Values Clarification technique," he says (1984, p. 78). Values education is *altering* one's character, not simply reinforcing it, Meilaender argues. It is offering admonition, training, instruction as to right and wrong ideas and behavior. Meilaender scoffs at "our fear of indoctrination, a word at least as bad as 'hypocrisy' in our moral vocabulary" (p. 79).

This debate is suggestive for a better understanding of our moral task as educators in the church. Just as we have argued in discussing counseling, assumptions are over-drawn about the possibilities of a teacher's being altogether neutral, of standing apart from all value positions. The methods of values clarification enable the teacher to ask helpful questions of the student: "Did you consider alternatives?" "What other possibilities were there?" "Would you be willing to tell others about that idea?" Each question rests on implicit values, such as the worth of weighing alternatives, or of sharing moral conviction in communal discourse.

Critics of values clarification may argue that the strategy inevitably uses leading questions and so represents its own form of indoctrination. Meilaender quotes an amusing illustration set forward by Richard Baer, one of the critics:

Student: Yesterday I poured blue paint all over my cat.
Teacher: How did you feel when that happened?
Student: I felt terrible. I should have used red paint.
Teacher: No. I meant, how did you feel about getting paint all over the cat?
Student: Oh. I felt terrible. I shouldn't have done anything to harm my cat. (p. 80)

Nonetheless, certain virtues of values clarification can be cited. The strategy recognizes that education is more than acquiring information. It is growth in values. Values clarification teaches that growth can be fostered by taking positions and defending them in open discussion. People may disagree. These are democratic values, and they are consistent with our earlier emphasis on autonomy. Values clarification teaches that inquiring into the facts of a case and considering other opinions is worth while. At a more sophisticated level, values clarification demonstrates that people have different traditions of value, different loyalties, different styles of reasoning.

On the negative side, particularly to be noted for church educators, values clarification seems to suggest that there is no objective order of value. One person's opinion or value seems to be as good as the next. It might be read to say that feelings are all that matter. It may be argued that values clarification is too optimistic about human nature.

"The trick," as Meilaender says, "is not to be morally neutral but to avoid whatever constitutes objectionable indoctrination." That, he suggests, is "the deliberate attempt at directly affecting the value system without . . . collateral legitimation to the recipient."[1]

---

1. p. 80. At this point Meilaender is quoting from Michael Scriven.

Objectionable indoctrination, that is, is coercive teaching that does not explain itself, does not give reasons. Objectionable indoctrination disallows autonomy; examples include brainwashing and subliminal advertising. "Good indoctrination" includes explanation, reasoned justification, and permission to proceed.

But what then of children, who do not yet have reasoning powers, who are not yet autonomous? Do we avoid teaching them values? The answer lies, it would seem, in a developmental gradient. We will not avoid teaching rules to younger children before their reasoning abilities are developed, but as children develop, we will increasingly coach and instruct them only with accompanying explanation and justification. We will proceed in dialogue that respects the inner reflective and intuitive capabilities of the children. If this gradient is not followed, or not followed early enough, the wrongness of indoctrination in the bad sense will eventually overwhelm whatever good may appear to result from the moral guidance.

The use of such a gradient is consistent with our understanding of moral development in children. In reporting his extensive research with children, Jean Piaget describes their early beliefs that rules—in the game of marbles, for example—have been given by adults from times immemorial, have never changed, and cannot change. Later, after the age of eleven or so, children come to realize that the rules are changeable and that they themselves might even experiment with changed rules, creating variations on the game. Young children can quite naturally accept "indoctrination"; they can be compulsive about rules, with little understanding. But once they are older, they know better. At the latter stage, that is, moral behavior and personal integrity depend on more than admonition. Piaget believes that the child of eight to ten develops an autonomous sense of justice, a mindset that replaces an earlier morality based on an unquestioning respect for adult authority. In a similar developmental sequence, Piaget demonstrates that younger children measure blame by the amount of material damage—in a story, for example, about a child who broke some cups. Only at age nine and later does intention seem important—whether the accident, for example, was unwitting or came about because a child was reaching for some forbidden jam when Mother was not looking. The younger child thinks of a lie as any misstatement of fact, whether by mistake or through intentional deception. The older child knows the difference.

Stage Theory for Moral Development

Recent researchers have picked up the pioneering work of Piaget in their own attempts to understand moral development. From his extensive research, with people of all ages, Lawrence Kohlberg perceives a process of development through "stages" or "levels" of moral maturation. This progression is to be found, he reports, even across cultures. The sequence of these steps is always the same, although the great majority of people do not reach the last two stages.

Lawrence Kohlberg's work is well known and needs only the briefest summary here. Basically, what Kohlberg does is to analyze the process of reasoning in people's answers to questions about moral dilemmas they are asked to decide. He says there seem to be six stages of development in moral reasoning, and he groups the six by pairs. Stage one and two he groups as "level one," which he calls the "preconventional" level, found mostly in children. The orientation here is to simple disobedience. At the first, "stage one," a child says that rules should be obeyed and decisions should be made to avoid punishment. At the second, the reason is to gain rewards. The next two stages compose a second "level" that Kohlberg labels "conventional." Here is to be found the behavior that conforms to social norms, with the reasoning in the first case that this is necessary for social approval, or, in the next stage, for social stability. A "post-conventional" level, also called a "principled" level, includes, in the first case, a stage in which there is an emphasis on the social contract and individual rights, and a second, in which one reasons from a sense of universal ethical principles, and from an appeal to personal conscience.

Building on both Kohlberg and Piaget, James Fowler (1981) has done research aimed at tracing the developmental sequence in patterns of religious faith. Again, there are six stages, somewhat paralleling those of Kohlberg. In terms of religious faith, after (1) an "intuitive/projective" stage characteristic of the young child, he finds (2) a "mythic/literal" stage of the eight-year-old to eleven-year-old. Then (3) there arises a "synthetic/conventional" stage of faith, when the child is eager to participate in the patterns of belief of significant others, as yet not ready to make many autonomous judgments of its own. The teen of seventeen or eighteen years of age may enter (4) an "individuating/re-flexive" stage, though some people never do, and many only in their thirties or later. This stage sees a collapse of naive acceptance of inherited faith and conventional norms. A person rejects or internalizes for himself or herself a variation of the older faith structures, and takes personal responsibility for beliefs, attitudes, and actions. In two later stages, the more mature person (5) will have thought through more of the enigmas of religious faith and can live more comfortably with paradox; and such a person (6) will have finally come to an even more universal love and loyalty, and is more deeply aware of the transcendent. Fowler can chart this sequence in biographies of respected persons and in narrative accounts of subjects he has interviewed in longitudinal studies.

There are marked similarities in Piaget, Kohlberg, and Fowler. They all describe the growth from "conventional" or accepted rules, morality, and "faith" into a stage that is more flexible and open. Moral maturity is the critical appropriation of tradition—of a culture's norms and reasoning—*for oneself*, taking into account one's own experience and reflection.

A number of critics have raised questions about stage theory. I shall cite two of them here. In essence, critics argue that stage theory is too schematized to deal with the subtleties of moral consciousness and behavior. Carol

Gilligan (1982) finds in Kohlberg, as well as in Piaget, an unconscious sexist bias. Girls and women, she finds, are often troubled by different aspects of a moral dilemma from what boys and men perceive, and they make responses that are less "logical." But they are equally sensitive in moral terms. They rate "lower" in a stage theory of development, but they are not morally less mature. For the female, the "moral problem arises from conflicting responsibilities rather than from competing rights and requires for its resolution a mode of thinking that is contextual and narrative rather than formal and abstract" (p. 19). For Gilligan morality is concerned with the activity of care, and she would center "moral development around the understanding of responsibility and relationships" rather than simply the concept of fairness, which "ties moral development to the understanding of rights and rules" (p. 19).

Robert Coles is a psychiatrist and writer who has done extensive research among children of migrants, the Southern poor, and slum dwellers of the Third World. Coles argues that we far too easily dismiss young children as lacking moral insight. Ruby Bridges, the best known of the children he describes, made a profound impression on him. She changed history as well. Ruby was the little black six-year-old who for months went to a "white" school in the early days of desegregation in the South, escorted by federal marshals through ranks of menacing hecklers. Ruby Bridges' courage and compassion went against all the psychological theory Coles brought to his research, theory that would expect her to break down, and would label her statements—such as those about praying for those who threatened her—"imitative behavior" copied mindlessly from some adult. Coles found them more profoundly rooted than that. Following children and youths over the years, Coles acknowledges that many of them invest a spirited moral energy in their inner struggles and possess an often mind-boggling integrity.

Children do not necessarily fit our stereotypes and categories. Coles has the gift of listening to them on their own terms. And on their own level, he finds moral passion.

He uses a discussion of movies, for example. Children may focus on a tiny episode in *Raisin in the Sun,* not on the big issue of radical justice but on how a mother ought or ought not to discipline her daughter. In thinking over *To Kill a Mockingbird,* instead of the courage of a heroic lawyer-father, a child celebrated the good character that this man's children find emerging in a neighbor who had at first seemed only strange and scary.

Coles says that in Kohlberg's scheme, Ruby Bridges "was a 'preconventional' or 'premoral' lass. Her prayers, her smiles, were, I suppose, mere gestures, not the careful responses of a truly reflective person" (p. 27). But in coming to know her, Coles found in her courage, compassion, and integrity much more than that.

There was little reflective logic, either, in the teenager who was the first white youth to speak to a black in the newly integrated Atlanta high schools. "He was from a family," writes Coles, "all too easily labeled, by the likes of me, 'redneck.' He was a tough athlete, a poor student, not a well-read boy of fourteen." He would not have fared well in a Kohlberg quiz. Yet after weeks when whites had offered only silence to blacks, on an occasion when whites were taunting a black, and threatening him, this fourteen-year-old intervened to prevent trouble, and then said to the black, "I'm sorry." The white youth explained, says Coles, "I didn't mean to, actually! . . . I was surprised to hear the words myself: 'I'm sorry.' . . . That was the strangest moment of my life" (p. 28). Soon, says Coles, the white youth was championing the black personally, while still decrying integration. "Finally, he would become a friend of the black youth and advocate 'an end to the whole lousy business of segregation.' "

Gilligan and Coles argue that morality is much more than moral reasoning. Kohlberg, for example, does his research by asking children and adults what should be done in the face of certain set moral dilemmas that the researcher presents, and why. He then classifies the answers, measuring, the critics would say, not so much morality as ability in moral logic. But morality is made up of empathy, compassion, intuitive hunches about fairness, and self-awareness, as well as ability for ethical reasoning. These elements play subtle and complex roles in the moral development of children. An eight-year-old I know confided to her mother one day she thought the teacher was choosing her to do too many things in school. "You're afraid it might make the other children feel bad," replied her mother; "You can tell your teacher that, if you want." "Well," said the child, "I kind of like it, too."

Part of the dilemma of moral education lies in this fact that ethical reasoning is not the same as moral virtue and action. Meilaender admits his own doubts about direct instruction in ethics. He quotes social analyst Mark Lilla, who fears that in college ethics courses, as in symposia for public officials, people "are learning a rather peculiar sort of philosophical discourse which allows them to make sophisticated excuses for their actions" (p. 75). Kohlberg himself stresses that morality is something different from being able to name the right and the wrong. He cites one of the early psychological studies of moral development, a study by researchers Hugh Hartshorne and M. A. May, involving 11,000 children. Six classes of children, for example, after three weeks of "honesty instruction" were, five to one, a little more deceptive than before the instruction. "Subjects who say that cheating is very bad or that they would never cheat are as likely to cheat in an experimental situation as are subjects who express a qualified view as to the badness of cheating." The authors conclude that a study of early training about honesty, blame, and the like is less likely to yield as much of an understanding of moral development as a study of more general experiences related to ego development and self-control under normal processes of growing up.

The Moral Nurture of Children

Mark Jones' hunches can serve him well. Sermonettes and moralism in church school classrooms do not create persons of integrity and compassion. How then can the church best serve to nurture the moral growth of children?

1. We may respond to the question in utter dismay. The church has but an hour a week for relating to most children, we may argue. How can it dream of significant influence on children, when a hundred other waking hours are subject to the sway of playmates and television and school?

A deeper reading justifies a more positive assessment. Religion can sustain for a people a symbolic universe far out of proportion to the hours spent under the roof of a church building. The power of the ritual rehearsal of meanings sets a framework for the Philbys and their children more pervasive than they may themselves imagine. Baptism has set an identity and marked a commitment. The holy days of the church year review the stories of Jesus. The social network of the church involves Linda and Nick in a supportive fellowship that strengthens a Christian inter-pretation of the human enterprise.

We have already referred to certain values that are legitimately fostered by the public schools, even in our secular, pluralistic society. The church is an intentional, confessional community that can go far beyond those democratic principles. Indeed, it may be argued that morality without a (religious) sense of transcendent grounding is shaky at best. The church does not stand over against the schools. It provides a richer, deeper grounding both for personal identity and for sparking the prophetic criticism needed by any society. St. Andrew's and every other parish church are a significant, indispensable part of the moral environment in which the Cheryl and Denny Philbys are to grow up.

2. We can begin by stating three convictions that grow from all the commentary above.

a. One's moral life is a function of the whole person. Our goal in education is not so much conformity to social norms as it is character, and virtue, and integrity. These things amount to much more than adherence to moral prescrip-tions and proscriptions. They arise from one's intention in, one's disposition toward, the world. They arise from one's inner faith, as opposed, possibly, to one's verbally professed beliefs. They are part of one's "functional theology," as opposed, possibly, to one's formal religious thought. It is easy to profess one belief system and behave in ways at odds with it. We see this in our own selves all too often.

b. Autonomy is a goal in education as it is in pastoral care and counseling. The autonomous person can cope with the new situations that aren't provided for in the rules, and is less confused by the tragic instances when one good must be chosen against another.

c. Rules and guidelines play a larger role in the moral life of the immature than the mature, but they are never altogether dispensable. Early, and increasingly, a child will be provided explanation and justification for moral admonition, and offered free choices as appropriate.

With Mark Jones' coaching, St. Andrew's can mature in its sense of purpose for its children. Its teachers will reflect on the fact, for example, that one's moral life is a function of the whole person. This means that teaching rules and principles to children is part of the more fundamental task of nurturing a selfhood generously disposed toward the world. The quality of relationship to parents, mentors, and friends is more important than the actual code that is taught. A heavy-handed enforcement of right "Christian" conduct can destroy the more fundamental goal of moral growth. It can defeat rather than nurture a child, making for fearfulness, stinginess, or self-righteousness.

The holistic approach to moral nurture means that a whole range of concerns comes into view, and a deeper sense of the environment we want to structure so as to foster moral development.

1. If a basic trust and confidence in life are a foundation for moral behavior, even the first weeks and months of an infant's life are part of its nurture toward generous concern for the neighbor. The child's needs must be dependably and lovingly met. Basic trust, fostered at this ego-centered stage of life, is the groundwork for later empathy, the ability to identify with and eventually reach out to others.

2. As the months pass, reinforcing a sense of reliability

and order in the environment, parents and teachers provide another aspect of moral nurture. Such simple steps as feeding an infant and putting a child to bed can mean both security and compliance with a schedule. Firm tenderness and loving structures are highly important to the development of a solid sense of self, and of personal identity. Thereby we also nurture the first understanding that not all private wishes can be fulfilled; we initiate wholesome internal attitudes that later counteract greed and exploitative relationships to others.

3. Later socialization in play and nursery school groups and in kindergarten is a third step in moral nurture. "Playing" is the main work of children at this age, more important than the cognitive achievements of first use of letters and numbers. Positive experiences of interaction with other children develop further the capacity to move beyond the ego-centeredness of infancy toward concern for the other. The rules of taking turns and sharing are only part of this experience. Simply having a good time alongside one another and, as time passes, in joint play, is equally important.

By responding to a child's behavior with appropriate praise or discouragement, parents and teachers lay early foundations for a child's own control of the self-centered impulses that are natural and necessary in the infant. These impulses need gradual conversion by the time of adulthood, for the sake of social participation and Christian service. Guidance is important. An avoidance of structure, based on the optimism of an ultraprogressive view of education, is more likely to lead to a community like that in *Lord of the Flies* than to a new paradise. Our stress on getting beyond conformity and onto the gradient toward autonomy does not imply a belief that a "natural," Rousseauean goodwill will prevail if only all culture-generated inhibitions be shucked off from infancy on.

In strong language, the well-known psychiatrist Bruno Bettelheim adds a psychoanalytic perspective to the importance of discipline in childhood. "The mistake we still make is to hope that more and more citizens will have developed a mature morality, one they have critically tested against experience, without first having been subject as children to a stringent morality based on fear and trembling" (in Gustafson et al., 1970, p. 87). The rules, consistently and dependably enforced in childhood, says Bettelheim, give the ego and superego the strengths they need for both cognitive and moral learning. Only on that basis will maturity and personal integrity develop.

The small child who is taught to think (or whose life experience teaches him) that taking things without permission is all right on some occasions but not on others will have a superego that is full of holes, one that will not later support him toward academic achievement. Kant's categorical imperative requires a maturity of judgment, an ability to step outside one's private world and appreciate the experience of others, which is not available to the young. . . . To the immature mind the sometimes yes and sometimes no means only that I can act as I please.

4. In the middle childhood years, affiliative relationships play a large role in moral development. The child of eight to twelve wants to be a part of a club. The lore of the group and the norms of the group, the rules of players in the game, can become important. Piaget lays great stress on the morality that is learned from group interaction, apart from adult requirement and instruction. Besides Brownies, Cub Scouts, and Boy Scouts, the church may offer its own acolyte, choir, and church school groups as affiliative opportunity. A strong sense of group identity, as long as it is open to newcomers without destructive prejudice, is useful. The games and other activities of the group provide practice in dealing with rules, and resolving disputes offers experience in role-taking, or dealing with more than one point of view. Norms taught in such a group should not be coercive, but pressure for rational criticism and personal reflection on the validity of ideals is as yet usually premature. However, if questions arise from children themselves, they should be dealt with seriously and with reasoned discussion. Suppressing the questioning defeats the long-range goal of a more autonomous and personal appropriation of moral values.

5. With the age of adolescence, when "formal operational" thinking is far more possible for the youth (this is Piaget's term, used in his fundamental work on cognitive development), a new world opens up for moral growth. Now ideas of love and truth and fairness can be understood to apply beyond one's own personal relations and beyond one's own group. The exercise of fairly formal moral reasoning on ethical dilemmas, for example, becomes more plausible. It can serve as one aspect of moral development at this stage. Kohlberg cites research he did with a colleague. They found an upward shift of one stage in a third of the classes given ethical instruction through discussing moral dilemmas. The control classes, untaught, remained unchanged. A year later, the experimental classes retained their relative advance over the others.

In adolescence, social criticism is in order wherever there are disadvantaged persons or moral inconsistencies in public life. The goal is not cynicism, of course, but moral growth. Pedagogically, the great challenge at this level of moral development is the move beyond inherited norms of good socialization and decent conventional behavior into a more committed passion for practicing justice and loving mercy. The process of schooling and, all too often, the pressures of parents themselves, are oriented toward personal achievement, toward personal, worldly success. The love of knowledge, art, and virtue for their own sake is underemphasized, and encouragement of a passion for justice or altruistic love of others, even at cost to oneself, is left to one side. Ethics is still taught as rules of social living, rather than as an integral part of one's faith, one's basic life stance.

We need an active, experiential kind of education, given that larger vision for Christian moral maturity. Helping others should be a regular experience for younger children in church. Singing carols to shut-ins, making and delivering favors for convalescent homes, and bringing canned goods for food pantries can be but the beginning. They should be satisfying experiences, even though they can also serve as an introduction to the realities of human suffering and need.

Adolescents can be more pro-active. Walkathons for hunger or UNICEF, picketing for peace, leafleting, writing to or meeting with legislators and business and labor leaders can follow. Teen groups will adapt some of the ideas found in the work camp movement and the Peace Corps, challenging genuine investment of self in meaningful, horizon-broadening service. Confirmation classes will learn about denominational effort at social change as well as aid for Third World development.

Moral education sees learning under three rubrics, not just two. There is the cognitive task, which involves the ability for ethical reasoning and the development of rudimentary social analysis and criticism. There is an affective task, instilling attitudes and feelings of good will and mutual respect. And there is also a conative task, helping youth toward investing their lives in service for others, in pursuing the shalom vision of the kingdom.

Erik Erikson (1965) argues that the greatest gift of youth, all too often ignored and unchallenged, is fidelity. Idealism and selflessness can surface in far more teens and young adults than the yuppie subculture would lead us to believe, were we to take Erikson's assertion seriously. Alfred North Whitehead once proposed that religion evolves through three stages: "From God the void to God the enemy, and from God the enemy to God the companion" (1926, pp. 16-17). In moral development, the young person grows from thinking of God as rule maker to God as guide and companion in the struggle for personal integrity, social justice, and peace.

The congregation's self-understanding, in moral terms, emphasizes both its roles as a healing, reconciling community for personal life, and as *laos* in mission and service for the world's shalom. A church's adult life should be saturated with reports of Christian social witness and service. Teens should be included in missional projects wherever possible. Those individuals who have found ways of turning their occupational life into obvious avenues of Christian service should be sharing their stories with younger members. The many debates and discussions of moral and public policy issues that will characterize this community of moral deliberation should be frequently designed partly with youth in mind. Youth are ready to sit in on debates about arms control, welfare and the poor, foreign aid, affirmative action, the sexual revolution, gun control, and the environment, especially among adults they already know. They may surprise their elders by speaking up, expressing their idealism. They are cognitively ready to do this kind of thinking, and attitudinally often more ready than their parents. If the church's and the culture's leadership is wanting, fidelity can waste away in an acquisitive secular environment.

In chapter 7 we will discuss one dimension of moral education, and the minister's moral counselor role in it. I select the field of sexual ethics, for several reasons. First, it is a problematic one for many clergy, who wonder how the norms relate to reality anymore, and how to teach and preach and counsel about sexuality in church. Second, it is an area for both wholesome, holistic nurture and explicit teaching, for the young and for the adult. Finally, it can serve, perhaps better than most, as an example of the range of issues in any single ethics area we might choose for the pastoral-moral counselor.

CHAPTER SEVEN

Application:
Human Sexuality

LOOK IN ON THE PHILBY FAMILY AGAIN AFTER A few years. Danny, now fifteen, is setting forth on his first "official" date. Linda and Nick smile—nervously—as he saunters off to meet a girl for a high school dance. They wonder what the evening holds out for him. They know the shyness hiding behind the big-guy bravado. They know that his date has a reputation for being a little fast. They feel they are already beyond the time they can do much for Danny's understanding of right and wrong in boy-girl things. He's so much on his own. His own peers seem to do most of the standard setting that shapes his life. "I feel the way most parents say they feel when they turn their kids loose for college," said Nick. " 'The die is cast now,' they tell me. 'We've succeeded in teaching some standards—or not succeeded; time will tell.' "

Cheryl Philby is twelve. She came to her mother a week ago to ask for help. Cheryl was beginning her first menstrual period, with all the uncertainty, worry, and pride of young womanhood that mix into the experience. Linda realized suddenly what a lot of background—wholesome, and unwholesome—contributed to the way Cheryl would experience and remember this moment. It had to do with how she felt about her own body, how she felt about herself as girl-on-the-way-to-being-woman, how she visualized being an adult—being married, loving and being loved, being a lover, and being a mother. Linda wondered whether the way she had related to Cheryl, and the way Nick had, had prepared her for growing up sexually. It had all come so soon.

Linda Philby and Nick ponder their children's adolescence with a wholesome perspective. They recognize the range of influences that contributes to the sexual attitudes and practices of their children, the church and the school among them. They know that sexual morality is much more than a kit-bag of do's and don'ts, but they have wanted clear standards for their children too.

The Mixed Voices That Guide Us

Not all our parishioners have as healthy-minded a perspective on human sexuality as the Philbys. And far from the majority of our youth and children have so solid a home—with its once-married, still-married father and mother team—to grow up in. Chances are that Danny and Cheryl will do all right, but many others, given their circumstances and given our culture, will not. Human sexuality is one of the most urgent of all the arenas for our moral counsel. It is also one in which the way for us to go is most confusing.

To understand the reasons for our befuddlement, we can return to our "force field" metaphor out of physics. The ordained minister works in the presence of many diverse influences and claims, as if pulled by various magnetic forces all at the same time. The various cultural and theological forces do not all tug at us from the same direction. The moral counselor needs to be aware of these forces.

Two historical changes begin the list, for example. They are facts to which we have yet fully to accommodate ourselves. Nonetheless, with generally positive value, they are part of our force field, and they shape our counsel.

1. The *psychological revolution* that dates from Sigmund Freud has taught us the virtues of a greater openness about

sexual matters. We speak far more candidly than did our Victorian forebears about pregnancy and puberty, about sexual intercourse and homosexuals, about birth control and orgasm. By and large this seems to have freed us considerably from sexual hypocrisy in polite society, and from many of the older neurotic sexual maladjustments in marriage.

2. The *contraceptive revolution,* beginning with the Pill, has profoundly advanced the ease with which parents can plan their families, while still strengthening the companionate purposes of marriage through the sexual relationship. It has also lowered the risks in promiscuity.

This double revolution has complicated the inherited code, however. Some people believe that open discussion of sex and an emphasis on freed up expression of emotion have advanced promiscuity among the young. Reliable birth control has destroyed one of the easier arguments used by a former generation to bolster its deeper religious position forbidding sex outside marriage. Taken together, and adding on the realities of a mobile, more secular mass society, in which traditional village-life restraints are loosened, these two changes have facilitated the much touted sexual revolution. Whether that shift is as great a change as is supposed, and whether or not on balance it is a net gain, we do cherish the greater freedom brought us by the two root facts that so largely account for it.

3. Building on the sexual revolution, a *media explosion* based largely on mass advertising and television, has left us swamped in a tide of culture that both publicizes and promotes a shallow physiological view of sex. This perspective seems to crowd out our cherished religious insight that sexuality is a dimension of the whole self. In seeking their profits, the entertainment media and advertisers exploit sex in ways that cheapen it, often denigrate women, and confuse the young. Witting or unwitting, most people are accomplices in this process, at least as consumers. Pornography, while a serious concern, is but a small part of the larger issue. The sexual revolution cannot be legislated or adjudicated away, even by the most reactionary of

legislatures and courts. Nor can it be preached away, even by the most conservative of pastors.

4. Another vector in the force field is the *liberation of women*. Though primarily a matter of justice for a group often automatically dealt poor cards in economic opportunity and social power, the women's movement bears on sexual ethics because women are blowing the whistle on the double standard—in sex and social opportunity alike. They will not remain in the purdah of kitchen and nursery and bridge club. They go to work. They demand a freedom of movement and self-development equal to that of men. The divorce rate has gone up partly because women found they could support themselves in their new-found competence and because, in their new-found self-respect, they will no longer knuckle under to domineering men. Again, the moral counselor can only celebrate the basic advances all this represents.

5. Most important, the *claims of Scripture* and the *Christian past* guide the work of the moral counselor as well. Much deeper than rules, this tradition portrays the God-given destiny of man and woman to be for each other, in companionship and in sexual union (e.g., Gen. 2:18, 24). It dignifies fidelity in marriage to the extent that it interprets the very faithfulness of God to Israel with the marital metaphor. The biblical tradition does not offer the literalist or legalist a single clear norm for an ethics of sex and marriage. It forbids adultery (Exod. 20:14), but it accepts as matter of fact polygamy and concubinage among the patriarchs. It rejoices in sexual love (Song of Solomon), but Paul encourages his single readers not to marry. In the Gospels, we read that sinners and prostitutes enter God's realm more easily than those who consider themselves more virtuous.

Moreover, the broader Christian ethic makes us value many of the historical changes we have named. They are not mere accidents of modernity. Christian roots of change sometimes take a long time to branch and flower. Slavery was practiced for centuries in Christendom while the Christian tradition was its latent opponent. Similarly, the liberation of women, equality in sexual relationships, and more affirmative views of sex in human life derive from concerns not only wholly compatible with but always latent within a Judeo-Christian sensibility that affirms creation, opposes hypocrisy, and sustains a passion for justice. Thus, the moral counselor must seriously evaluate the entire force field in evolving sexual ethics. No part of it should be dismissed out of hand by a narrow traditionalism.

An Urgent Matter

In light of this welter of values and norms around sexual attitude and practice, one minister may be tempted to react with a renewed legalism and another to give up on moral reflection and say anything goes—if it does not obviously and directly hurt someone.

However, too many people are being hurt indirectly by a confused and weakened sexual ethic, one to which such lazy intellectual attitudes contribute. The AIDS crisis, the most serious venereal epidemic since the miracle drugs took on syphilis, and potentially far worse, is but the latest sign of urgency. Families fall apart in casual divorce, often leaving behind permanent emotional scar-tissue in the lives of vulnerable children, deserted spouses, and injured friendships. Teenagers develop promiscuous habits that lay little foundation for lives of sexual responsibility and personal fulfillment in marriage. Abortion, while permissible in certain circumstances according to most Protestant moralists, evolves into what amounts to another means of birth control, a trend opposed by the moralists. Teenage pregnancy, with the far-reaching physiological and emotional problems inflicted on children of child mothers and absent fathers, increases.

The urgency comes also from a distinct part of our American polity that lays a heavy burden on church and synagogue. As we have said, the separation of church and state has engendered, in our pluralistic culture, a certain timidity in the public schools when it comes to values. It is safe for a teacher to instruct about the biology of sex—relatively safe. But it is risky and more difficult to teach about standards of sexual conduct and human values. The easy way is therefore to teach the one and avoid the other. That very imbalance contributes to an instrumental, merely physiological understanding of human sexuality. Trying to mold the sexual morality of public-school students by inculcating one or another set of religious principles is against the law, to be sure. But a teacher even finds it difficult to make factual points *about* the various religious norms. Religious norms and arguments remain areas of ignorance for vast numbers of unchurched children and youth.

Of course, the urgency does not come to most pastors primarily in abstract language about social problems. It comes in events of parish life. Two youth leaders describe their sense of inadequacy after a teenage retreat; they had come upon two of their charges, a fifteen-year-old boy and a fourteen-year-old girl half naked and involved in heavy petting in one of the cabins. A male parishioner reports his affair with a secretary, asking for help as he tries to disentangle himself. A high school junior is pregnant, and a family is in crisis. A woman of twenty-three years of married life is suddenly deserted by her husband, who wants his "freedom"; she thinks their sexual relations have been part of the problem, and she wants help toward reconciliation. In a moment of candor and puzzlement, a sixteen-year-old asks if it is all right to sleep with her boyfriend, if they use birth control. A women's committee, preparing for a rummage sale, is heard talking about the "evils" of homosexuals and their clamor for equal rights. A boy in confirmation class says he feels terribly guilty over masturbation.

Getting Started

The pastor has a fourfold task in dealing with such a variety of experience in ministry. One part of that task is to achieve personal clarity about the moral dimension of sex and sexual responsibility. Another is to develop a framework or style for church counsel and program. A third is to activate the program. A final task involves referral, making the decisions about what is appropriate for the church and its pastor to undertake and what is not.

A minister should be able to articulate a theologically grounded sexual ethic for himself or herself. It will help to have worked through one or more theological books on sexual ethics. As we have argued earlier in this book, relying on pop psychology is not enough, not if we pretend to be practicing Christian ministry. Beyond the books, most denominations also have published resource materials, and several have enacted pronouncements about their own denominational consensus on sexual morality.

Beyond prayer and study, a good way of working at clarity of thought is writing. As honestly as possible, and in light of the complex factors of today's sexual environment, the pastor may try to set forth a contemporary Christian position. I can imagine a pastor writing in a journal, for example, something like the following paragraphs.

Conviction #1. Human sexuality is a gift of God. It is not something to be ashamed of. Sexuality is far more than sexual intercourse; it affects and enriches many human relationships. The human yearning for personal closeness and intimacy is related to and expressive of our yearning for the wholeness, communion, and well-being we associate with religious faith. "At last, bone of my bone, flesh of my flesh!"

Human sexuality has an indispensable role in the continuing life of the race and in filling out the destiny of man and woman, who are called into being for each other (Karl Barth). This destiny is symbolized in the creation story itself (Gen. 2:18-25). "It is not good that the man should be alone." "Therefore a man leaves his father and his mother and cleaves to his wife, and they become one flesh."

A merely repressive view of sexuality is not fundamentally biblical. Think of the Song of Solomon!

Rightly expressed, sexuality leads not only to pleasure, but also to profound joy.

Conviction #2. At the same time, sex can be an enormously powerful, self-centered drive in people. Therefore it is easily perverted with cruelty and exploitative manipulation of others, with self-indulgence at others' expense, or with shallow sensuality. No one is immune to disappointment and hurt in entering this quest for intimacy. Casual sex and slipshod theology about sex take these possibilities far too lightly. Paul makes our physical bodies "members of Christ" (I Corinthians 6), and on that basis forbids making them "members of a prostitute." The body is a "temple of the Holy Spirit." "Glorify God in your body," he says.

Conviction #3. Reasoning from convictions #1 and #2 makes responsible Christian teaching about sex an urgent matter. Given our society, it is also difficult—for the church, and for parents. The difficulty derives not only from the sensate culture around us, but also from a desire to affirm some aspects of the sexual revolution. It also derives from our Christian awareness of the mysterious power of sex for profound human communion and for "co-creating," with God, new human life. The "shame" that comes with the Fall (Gen. 2:25; 3:10) marks our remembrance of the mystery as well as the loss of innocence.

Conviction #4. Making a good marriage is part of the Christian calling for most people. Marriage dignifies sex. Sex can undergird and reinforce marital commitment and family stability. Culturally conditioned though it is, this view nonetheless also has solid grounding in both Scripture and Christian tradition.

Conviction #5. For other people—singles, homosexuals, the divorced, and the widowed—the Christian community should be a wholesome help rather than a problem, in pastoral care and in pronouncements on sex.

Conviction #6. The sexual revolution has left the church's traditional teaching either in a shambles or, where it is offered in legalistic, puritanical terms, largely unheeded and theologically inadequate to the times.

Approaches to the Task

Listening to culture and tradition, and articulating conviction are only part of pastoral action. As every pastor who is serious about the role of moral counselor knows full well, there is far more to the pastoral task of guidance and care than knowing theological argument and being able to recite church law. Moral growth is no simple cognitive matter. We easily fail to do the good we know in our minds (Romans 7).

The next pastoral task is to develop one's framework for counsel and program. Our earlier chapters have laid the groundwork for pastoral leadership in this area. The following comments carry those perspectives into the realm of sexuality.

1. Avoiding controversial or awkward moral issues is no solution. In terms of sexuality, avoidance is retreat. The culture is saturated with portrayals of manipulative and irresponsible sexual relationships. Young people watch and read enough to easily assume these are normal—and moral—unless church and school and home present a better way. The myth-making, world-forming common denominator for the broadest public now is probably not religion but television. T.V. soap operas average one sexual reference or act every nine minutes, with unmarried sex three times more common than married.

Permissiveness is actively promoted by advertisers and others for economic gain. The church's silence can be understood to mean one of two things: In the modern, liberated world, sex is no longer a moral and religious concern, or, the repressive "thou shalt not" body-spirit dualism of so much in the tradition is the major Christian view. In the latter case, today's youth and many others will largely dismiss the church as irrelevant because they find in it no help for their questions and their sense of sexual need. Yet the church wants to help people make decisions in sexual matters within a Christian framework. The best way for that is involvement with the young in nurture and education on human sexuality, and in moral counsel with adults.

2. In moral counsel, our more fundamental concern is attitude. Sexually, respect for a partner is far firmer ground for a good relationship than simply knowing rules of conduct. All interpersonal behavior has expressive and symbolic meaning to those involved. No relationship is "purely physical." In sex, this means that affection, gentleness, patience, commitment, and love are more basic than technical information on physiology. So too is a healthy appreciation of one's own body, and of oneself as a responsible person, in a meaningful, moral life. Sex education inevitably carries with it one implied set of moral meanings or another.

3. The ideal can be presented in ways that do not destroy rapport with those who hold to other standards. Paul was able to write about his preferences of celibacy without rejecting marriage, even marriage to non-Christians. Jesus taught sexual faithfulness within marriage, without rejecting the adulterer.

In counseling and teaching youth and young adults, most clergy and youth leaders will teach a standard of delaying sexual intercourse until loving, lifelong commitments are made, knowing full well that many will either disagree with that standard or fail in their hope to live up to it. That fact does not mean this ideal should not be presented; nor does it mean the church's teaching role and the terribly imperfect day-by-day response of Christians to that teaching are all a charade. Ideals do not evolve from surveys of behavioral majorities. We teach truthtelling, for example, knowing all the while of our own failures at it and even of occasions when hedging on truth is the better moral choice.

An expression of personal conviction is often the right move in pastoral counseling, but sometimes not. A developing rapport and the parishioner's autonomy can be sabotaged by untimely interventions or imperious advice. Factual reporting on the moral positions of the Christian community can be one non-judgmental tactic. The counselor may say at an appropriate point, "I think it will help in this discussion to remember that the church has generally taught sexual abstinence until marriage," or, "Yes, some conservative denominations call masturbation sinful, but you won't find that view in our own teaching materials."

A pastor may want to tell a closeted and troubled homosexual that some churches and many Christian moralists consider sexual orientation a matter of created destiny rather than wrong moral choice, and that, moreover, some consider celibacy the responsible choice in light of the orientation and others approve a long-term and committed homosexual relationship similar to marriage. A couple coming for premarital counsel, should they be asking for sexual guidance, have a right to know both that the church has recommended premarital abstinence and also that in the eyes of most moralists, the date of the wedding ceremony is less important than establishing personal and public commitment as a foundation for deepening sexual involvement.

Considering all the other influences on people, such information will seem only a small factor in decision making. Coming at a serious moment, however, and from an authority figure, it may far outweigh that estimate in its importance. At any rate, information is a part of the basis on which a person makes decisions.

4. Moral realism requires instruction and guidance about the less-than-perfect. In the ideal world, one would not need to instruct soldiers about the moral limits of "just war." There would be no war. In our world, we do. In the ideal world, one would not need to instruct twelve and thirteen-year-olds in methods of birth control, of "safe sex." None of them would be irresponsibly active in sexual matters; there would be no AIDS. Given the sexual activity of children in this society, we do. Sensitive, responsible, morally aware instruction about human sexuality or contraception will not accelerate a young person's drift into deepening sexual involvements. More likely the opposite. But even if it did, the matter is too urgent to avoid, whether

the instruction comes from home or school or church. Planned Parenthood reports that 20 percent of our thirteen and fourteen-year-olds are sexually active. A study of church-active youths thirteen to fifteen shows that one in eight has engaged in sexual intercourse, as have more than half the males sixteen to eighteen years old and about 40 percent of the girls (Clapp, 1985). Youths have a right to information about actual sexual practices, for example, to counteract misinformation from the street, or generalizations like "everybody does it." They also need instruction and support in the ability to say no when they are being pushed beyond their own level of sexual and emotional maturity, and beyond their convictions of the moral good.

5. Respect for autonomy means that rules need reasons, as early as they can be understood. This principle applies to sex as much as to any other sphere. A young person's appreciation of his or her sexual drive and the postponement of full coital relationship until marriage are not incompatible, given the psychological and moral reasons for waiting until both personal identity and affectional bonding are present. Reasons are highly important if this is to be understood and followed out by a teenage youth. A simple "No, the Bible says so," or "No, because adults say so," will not suffice for long into the teens. Adults and parents need to be evolving out of the disciplinarian roles as their sons and daughters take on responsibilities for themselves. As Nick's friend put it, "The die is cast" by the mid to late teens, given the freedoms of our society. One adult guide for Christian sex educators put it this way: "A sixteen year old should not be a parent in our culture, . . . but a sixteen year old should be exercising more decision-making power than is often extended to him in our culture" (Clapp, 1985, p. 32).

Occasions for Moral Guidance

The third pastoral task is initiative for program development. With the above perspectives in mind, the moral counselor discovers in congregational life a wide range of possibilities for nurture and instruction in human sexuality. For reasons already cited, teaching and moral counsel must take place well beyond the privacy (and inefficiency) of one-on-one pastoral care. The most available occasion, of course, is in preaching. Most congregations will be deeply grateful for thoughtful topical preaching, as much as twice a year, dealing with human sexuality in the light of faith.

The difficulty at this point is not the problem of speaking about sex in a sermon. With a little care, we can discuss most moral issues quite openly these days, even with children present. Magazines and television programs that regularly enter parishioners' homes have taken care of that. The difficulty is in the wide range of concerns among Sunday morning parishioners. In a congregation of any size, there are teenagers and the elderly, single and divorced and married, heterosexuals and, whether known or not, probably one or more homosexuals; and similarly, known or not, incest survivors and battered women. Therefore our treatment of specific sexual issues will generally illustrate some broader theological or ethical perspective, or open up a biblical text, rather than pretend to offer direct personal counsel in the manner of a call-in psychologist's radio or T.V. show.

Of itself, addressing sexual issues rather than tiptoeing around them makes several points. It says that Christian faith is concerned for all areas of our lives, not an isolated Sunday compartment. It suggests that people in the community of faith care enough about one another and about cultural norms that they explore together difficult, evolving areas of morality. It shows the preacher's pastoral concern. (Marie Fortune tells of a minister who, on returning from a short workshop on domestic violence, simply mentioned the trip in a sermon. Nothing more. The following week, he had three requests for help with problems of wife-battering in homes where he had had no inkling of the problem. Similar reports, especially from pastors who mention sex issues in the presence of teenagers, are common.)

A number of other teaching options present themselves,

some of them allowing considerably more depth than preaching does. Most pastors will find such elective subjects as "Christian faith and today's morality," or "sex and the Bible" attractive to continuing classes and study groups, or to ad hoc gatherings for short-term learning. An entire adult retreat can be programmed around such a theme. Some groups may want a systematic review of theological sexual ethics; others will want to back into religious perspectives by starting with contemporary problems—sex education in the schools, teenage pregnancies, the abortion controversy, the AIDS crisis, homosexuality. Couples' support groups, with their own systems of introducing topical discussions meeting by meeting (Becker, 1965) will evolve toward levels of trust that can easily handle discussions of sex ethics.

Parents' groups are of special importance. Many parents need help in simply talking about sex with their children. Some want help in establishing common rules and norms for their children, and interpreting Christian values to their adolescents, now so open to diverse influences and standards from their peer culture. Moreover, parent groups provide an excuse for some who want to probe issues of value and sexual relationships for themselves, but are insecure or shy about it. An examination of manuals for church sex education of children and youth can make for an interesting and useful evening of sharing by such a group.

Another strategic adult group is the cadre of church school teachers. Moral counsel by the pastor is multiplied through the church's teachers. Too many clergy, grateful to have discovered one program arm of the church that is capable of running itself, avoid involvement with the church school. Although week-by-week management may be left to others, the responsibility for teacher development should claim serious attention from one ordained as "pastor and teacher." Annually, one of the monthly meetings of the teaching staff, for example, might be given to discussing sexuality, or a whole day-long workshop might be given once every two years. Like other themes for staff development, this one should be primarily concerned for building responsible adult understanding. The teachers have their adulthood in common, even if the ages of the persons they teach vary greatly. If it is a sizable staff, subgrouping may then be helpful for dealing with questions of method and content for different age groups.

In a typical parish, there are three program options for direct work with youth participants. The first is the regular teaching program. The onset of puberty brings significant potential for reflection and spiritual development, as well as for emotional trauma. Junior high children should find the church program sensitive, caringly aware of their insecure quest for a new adolescent status. The curriculum in the church school should include acknowledgment of physical changes and units on emotional and spiritual growth, social skills, and the grounding of standards for boy-girl relations. As in all education, no one should assume that an area of learning, once covered, need not be dealt with again. The spiral learning pattern, in which subject areas are treated again and again at levels of greater and greater complexity, is best. Sexuality, in other words, will be a continuing study area later too, in high school age seminars and in adult study groups.

A second opportunity comes with confirmation education. Often, confirmation means direct teaching by a pastor, at least during some of the course. Depending on the age of the confirmation group, here is a unique occasion for trust-building and guidance. Thinking of ourselves as moral counselors will help. Alongside such concerns as faith and doubt, service and self-seeking, peer pressures and integrity, and parent relations, mutual discussion around questions of sexual growth and responsibility will help the trust to grow. This does not mean that the learning of Bible, history, liturgy, and Christian thought is unimportant. Confirmation, however, should be seen as the ingrafting of new participants into a faithful spiritual-moral community more than a polishing of candidates for a Bible quiz. We learn Scripture and Christian lore for the purpose of fostering the deepest possible participation in the community of faith.

Using anthropological models, one church has developed confirmation training into a demanding two-year pattern of "initiation into adulthood," with several rituals of separation, of testing stamina, and of exploring culture before a final return to the community, and church membership. Their four areas of study and personal growth—their four "journeys into understanding"—include units on society, the self, sexuality, and spirituality (Roberts, 1982).

Finally, youth fellowship activities—at both junior high and high school age levels—provide further opportunity. Well led, these offer a safe place not only for wholesome socialization into boy-girl activity, but also for explicit questions and answers on sexual issues, and, more important, for a discussion of values and theological frameworks that is unlikely to take place in the public school. Group life is an important occasion for growth toward committed, responsible adulthood, toward self-management in the radical freedom of the post–high school world. Most teen fellowships, for example, can be trusted to develop effective norms of behavior if they are asked to set standards in advance of a weekend retreat. They know the difficulties presented to the group by couples who pair off and withdraw, just as they know those of drugs and alcohol, and they will set appropriate norms. This is not a call for weak leadership or a "whatever you want" style of church guidance. Leaders themselves may have to establish norms in the loose or demoralized group.

Given this kind of atmosphere with youth, premarital counseling for the same people follows quite naturally as a further step of relationship to a pastor. For the more numerous couples who come to most clergy without this close a relationship, the leader's experience in such programming will facilitate his or her competence in the counseling.

Referral

The fourth task for the moral counselor is understanding the limits to what the church can and should attempt. The congregation is a public community, not an array of intimate, confidential therapy groups. If a parishioner asks for personal help around fetishism, child abuse, wife beating, or other problematic or perverse behavior, referral to clinical specialists is called for. This is not a rejection of the parishioner. Counseling contact is maintained, at a pace less intense than that of the therapist. Such referral is itself an act of pastoral caring—for the sick parishioner, and for the victims of his or her irrational sexual behavior. Some states require by law that child abuse be reported. No pastor should assume that the norms of confidentiality somehow excuse his or her failure to get an abuser into treatment through firm referral and follow-up.

Marriage counseling is undertaken by many competent pastors on a short-term basis. Referral to a marriage counselor in this case usually comes about because of constraints on the minister's time. In the event of such referral, the religious resources represented by the clergy-person must still be accessible—the caring community, the grace of prayer and the sacraments, the power of forgiveness and reconciliation, the norms of fidelity. Out of counseling sight must not mean out of touch or out of intercessory mindfulness.

CHAPTER EIGHT

Moral Counseling on Work-World Ethics

MOST ADULTS LIVE IN THREE "WORLDS." MORAL concerns are a dimension of life in each one of them. Adults live in the midst of families or an intimate circle of friends. They follow a civic and leisure-time life involving religion, play, and voluntary activities. And they work. How does the moral counselor relate his or her ministry to the world of work?

Owing to the social placement of most church activity and most pastoral service, clergy need far more awareness of the workplace than they come by naturally. Church life falls into the leisure time sector; it mostly occurs on the weekend, "suburban" sector of the week's routine, away from the workweek and workplace, away from the economic and political concentrations of power in the central city. It is more involved with personal and family concerns than with the public world. Because of all that, clergy usually associate religious and moral concern with these private life-spheres more than they do with the moral concerns that permeate the work-world.

This mindset, of course, is fallacious. Prophetic religion is as concerned for justice and human well-being in one arena as the other. Amos attacked corrupt merchants who made the "ephah small and the shekel great" (8:5) as much as he did the personal stinginess of the "cows of Bashan," religious infidelity, and oppressive statecraft.

Lay men and women, naturally enough, are subject to the same distorted sense of primary locus in religious and moral concern. They think of clergy as appropriately helpful for family life and community affairs in the residential neighborhood, but not for problems of the workplace.

The reasons for this go far beyond the matter of sociological and psychological "location." Consider but three additional factors. First, many of the ethical issues in business and the professions are complex. They are specific enough to each particular occupational field that they seem easily beyond the ken of a pastor. People may trust the minister with serious discussion of moral issues in family life or civic affairs. People have far less trust in a minister's counsel in matters pertaining to work. There, the parishioner is expert.

Furthermore, a pastor usually leads a group that is vocationally highly mixed. In the congregation may be plumbers and mechanics, salespeople of several sorts, lawyers and nurses and teachers, homemakers and students and building contractors, accountants and lab technicians and managers in various enterprises. The preacher for such a congregation cannot avoid speaking in generalities that seem not to address most of the job-specific ethical quandaries confronted by each of these persons in the diversity of the work-world. The nurse may be torn by doubt over an instance of passive euthanasia, the teacher by jealousy of a colleague who took credit for that teacher's ideas. The plumber is wondering whether he's right in refusing to strike alongside other union members, and the accountant has been asked by an important client to do a little "creative bookkeeping" to shave off some taxes. The construction contractor wants to keep the employees at work rather than laid off, which seems possible only by cutting dishonest corners to meet competitors who do the same in their own bidding. The manager struggles to decide about dismissing a chronic absentee whose family needs the job's income for its survival. No minister can easily hold such broad diversity in mind while attempting to make contemporary moral sense derived from ancient biblical texts. Generalizations can turn into platitudes that seem grossly unrelated to on-the-job ethics. Add that experience to the listeners' conscious and subconscious wish to quiet down their troublesome struggles of conscience, and we can see how easy it is for most lay people to exclude this work-world sector from moral concern: "Business is business."

There is a third reason for the well-known gap between business and the clergy, a gap that also pertains to the work of many outside the business world. We address this problem later, but I name it here as well. By training and emotional bent, we of the ordained ministry tend to think in global terms. Most workers in business, the trades, and even the professions think more specifically about particular pressures on the job. The mindset of professionally religious people develops universal principles of right and wrong; the other mindset thinks constantly of how to get the job done best, quickest, most efficiently, most profitably. The one is tempted to think in sweeping categories—all people should do such and such; the other thinks more concretely: "In our business we do this because it saves time and it works." The first viewpoint is idealistic: "Jesus says be selfless; the prophets say be just." The other thinks, "That doesn't help me keep my job (or meet the payroll, or ask for a raise, or decide whether or not to strike, or take the case, or make the risky investment)."

One teacher of business ethics uses the Kohlberg scheme discussed earlier (ch. 6) to explain the communication problem at this point. Our style of thought is in "stage six" says the ethicist, and the business-person's is likely to be at stage three or four. We talk past each other.

These various situational realities make for failure in moral counsel. The church and its pastoral leaders fall short of becoming significant resources for the moral struggle people experience in their work.

I can illustrate the difficulty lay people have in these matters with a story of two encounters I have reported elsewhere (Rossman and Noyce, 1985, p. 107; Noyce, 1981, pp. 802ff.). I told about a man I will call Marty Sams, a public-spirited man of great integrity and compassion. Attending a meeting in which someone had introduced the texts from Jesus about laying down life in service to others,

Marty said with some agitation, "I think I can serve my neighbor in my church work and in my civic involvements. I do a lot of that. At work, however, I must be self-centered, self-seeking." Someone tried to explain away the tension: "But in your earning you are serving your family." Marty Sams, however, would have none of it. "No, in my work I have to be selfish." For Marty, the indispensable profit-seeking in business did not fit into the gospel perspective.

A few weeks later, I was talking with a small-scale entrepreneur who was also a dedicated churchman, at that very time giving hours upon hours to a regional spiritual renewal campaign of his denomination. When I told him about Marty Sams, he was quick to agree: "Unfortunately, he is right. The only way to get along in business is to elbow your way forward more aggressively than the next person. You have to be able to kick and push the others more than they kick and push you."

The ethical concerns we encounter in the work-world range from the global to the seemingly petty. A manager in a transnational corporation touches issues of justice for the Third World. A metallurgist in a defense plant ponders the morality of nuclear weaponry. A university researcher helps sustain (or erode!) the tradition of integrity in scientific inquiry and free expression. A sales representative wonders about a padded expense account. A clerk considers calling in sick so as to have a day off.

We may organize most of the issues for ordinary work-world ethics under five sets of relationships—those to other employees, to the organization, to the economy and the consumer, to the environment, and to the law. One can be self-centered to the point of harming others in each of these arenas, or more principled and just and caring. Beyond these ranges of reflection and action, there are other profound moral issues peculiar to various occupational sectors, such as those in medical ethics, or in government and law. There is also a more fundamental kind of ethical discussion, an analysis of the assumptions upon which the whole work-world stands—the ideological structure of the economy, of social relations, and of government.

Two Theological Assertions

The first of the areas listed above, relationships with fellow employees, can illustrate an axiom of work-world counseling and two of the theological assumptions on which we must proceed.

The axiom has to do with freedom and power. One's moral ties to peers and colleagues at work, to subordinates and to superiors, are all human ties. They can contribute to the quality of group life, or erode it. A person can conscientiously attempt to affirm and assist a co-worker, can neglect such a relationship, or can denigrate others for the sake of personal gain. Ministers hear more of these problems than of those in the other sectors because, since human relationships are involved, these problems are part of the main agenda in personal counseling. They are also therefore part of that assumptive world of "legitimate" religious concern.

Intending the good for others at the workplace cannot be acted out so easily as in neighborhood and family relationships. The workplace is more structured by norms. of authority, responsibility, formal job descriptions, time constraints, profit-making, "turf." One's position is so confined that many people in both management and on the line feel powerless; they say they have no freedom for moral purpose. Their constraining field of forces feels like a prison. Therefore, their work is amoral, they say; it lacks moral dimension. "It's just a job."

Just here is the first sentiment against which moral counsel can be directed. Our axiom? Everyone, in one way or another, has *some* degree of power—power at least to attempt moving toward an interpersonal ethos of integrity and personal concern with peers. One man said, "There are only thirty people where I work, but I could disappear from the face of the earth some day and I don't think anyone would care, or maybe even notice." Any employee could begin to change that.

People in management experience the same kinds of frustrations as those on the line, although they usually possess wider discretionary freedom for the exercise of influence and power. But at all levels the axiom holds. Restricted as the options are, everyone has some degree of power. That power is to be identified; it is the first basis of moral reflection and action.

The first of two theological assumptions implicit in the discussion to this point is this: Every one of us lives within structures that *inhibit* our freedom of movement. We are created in community, and that means we act within constraints and limits. These are simply the boundaries we encounter because of other persons' rights and needs. In a civilized and developed society, there arise innumerable norms, regulations, precedents. This helps explain why so many people feel boxed in. Many of the rules make no obvious sense, but it is clear too that one contravenes them at risk of position or even one's entire livelihood. "Deep description" of the norm, like that of an anthropologist (cf. Geertz, 1973), can usually reveal some utility in the norm—for the good of the firm, the profession, or the economy. (Although a quick and energetic brickmason, for example, would reap temporary personal advantage by "busting the rate," such a mason would not do so, in deference to slower buddies. Such foot-dragging can frustrate a manager who provides piece-work incentives and sees the slowdown as immoral. For the workers, the long-term advantages of the practice are obvious.) Whether or not the rules are functional, however, and whether or not they need reform, such ordering habits and structures of life set limits to our freedom.

A second theological assumption is this: Every structure is morally *ambiguous*. To put it another way, sin abounds. This means that whatever innovations are made in a workplace, whatever improvements and reforms, we do not think of them as final. We are not to idolize any scheme—laissez faire, profit-sharing, worker-ownership, socialist, or capitalist—as the kingdom. All systems, including the economic system and the workplace, are under judgment, subject to reform and renewal. We are always to keep watch for openings toward their further humanization.

The moral challenge the counselor can always have in

mind—therefore, the challenge to people like Marty Sams—is the assignment of simply chipping away, facing morally forward. This chipping away is the Christian calling, not the realization of a moral utopia. It is important to put the matter in these terms because, lacking this understanding, a morally serious person may find the impossibility of moral innocence or large-scale reform to be devastating. He or she may end up callous, or overcome with despair, or evolving toward the cynical view that moral concerns do stop at the workplace door. Chipping away means righting wrongs where possible, enhancing the moral quality of workplace community, and reaching for the larger innovations and reforms as occasion arises. Reinhold Niebuhr's aphoristic prayer is appropriate: "God grant me the serenity to accept things I cannot change, courage to change things I can, and wisdom to know the difference."

Beyond these two theological assumptions, it is important that the pastor have in mind an intellectual framework that can undergird his or her work-world counsel. The moral counselor in this arena needs a social ethic. It may be liberationist, reformist, or sociologically functionalist. In economics it may lean toward left or right. There is no one Christian conceptualization of the social system. But people need to sense that their work fits into a pattern of meaning.

Let us say that Nick Philby comes in to talk to his pastor one day about the meaninglessness of his work, his frustrations from being "stuck," his sense that he is just pushing papers and getting nowhere, and his ethical disagreements with the boss. With no particular plans, he thinks about quitting. Mark Jones will listen of course, deeply aware himself of the emptiness of much work, and its moral ambiguities. In all probability Nick will develop for himself a sense of direction in the sorting-out process of some pastoral conversations. But against what background of assumptions shall Mark be listening? If Nick's is a cynical despair genuinely born of pressures for moral compromise, Mark's thinking might run as follows: At very least, work provides bread and butter for the table. That is a beginning of meaning. Beyond that, work may constitute an outlet for human creativity, for making things, or making things happen. It can be an avenue for aesthetic satisfaction, for communication with others. Work is a means of participating in the social order. It forms one more nexus, beyond the family and civic neighborhood, for the building of the human community. Combined with the efforts of others, work serves the social and economic well-being of the race. And in some small way, chipping away at the moral problems is our vocation. Nick may move, but he will not be free from moral struggle; that problem will accompany him.

Mark Jones will respect Nick's work for its moral value in at least one of these areas, without demeaning it because it is not morally more important or more innocent. When Nick reports that his work does not seem "meaningful," Mark will anticipate his depression. He knows how much the identity of a person in our society comes from work. Mark is cautious about the "quitting" part, for he knows that the unemployed person in our society can lose enormously in self-respect, personal satisfaction, and self-confidence, much as this may be hidden from public view.

Mark knows we may serve broader values in our work as well. Workers on the medical team serve health; the legal system, justice; governmental workers, the polity; managers, the economic well-being of society; parents, the upbringing of children; teachers, the handing on of a culture and the pursuit of knowledge. Eventually, he would like to help Nick find work in which he could find some such fundamental meaning.

Arenas of Moral Concern in Work

A sampling of issues will illustrate the range of pastoral conversation in relation to the work-world, and it will heighten our moral sensitivity. The central pastoral goal is not the righting of particular wrongs; it is developing heightened moral sensibilities in the parishioner, and heightened motivation. The parishioner is the expert who knows the patterns and problems in a given secular line of work, not the pastor.

The first arena, as put forth earlier, is that of relationships to fellow employees. We should encourage growth toward principled behavior, beyond mere self-preservation and self-seeking. This involves respect for the personhood of others, even when disagreements are profound, or when policy is unjust. The norms of fairness and justice apply to relationships with peers, subordinates, and superiors.

The second arena, we suggested, is relationship to the organization. We live in an organizational society. Nearly 95 percent of us work for an organization; few are self-employed, even among the professionals of medicine and law (Alperovitz, 1984). The issues here are legion. Beyond reliable and competent work, what is the employing organization's due? (Must young managerial families be uprooted every three to five years for the sake of corporate welfare?) What other loyalties must be given up in deference to the organization? (Large corporations are like little governments; they control a large part of employees' lives. What then is due process, and what are the "civil liberties" of the governed?) One's life being so influenced by the system, are there adequate means for participating in its governance? (Is there free speech? May the individual employee criticize the firm when on and off duty?) Is the employer sexist, racist, or otherwise prejudiced against certain groups?

If work has moral meaning, reducing organizational decision making to money criteria alone is wrong. The moral counselor may help both managers and employees question such oversimplification. Does not a worker build a moral claim to a job from years of serving in that capacity, beyond the specified wages and benefits paid month by month? Upon termination, should these moral claims to long-standing blue collar jobs be bought back from workers with "parachutes" like those of managers? What does the company owe in the way of enhancing satisfaction on the job? These questions go beyond enlightened corporate self-interest. "Oughts" are involved. Labor law only begins to specify some of the broad moral concerns of parties to workplace arrangements.

A third arena, equally complex, is that of relationships to the economy and the consumer. Here are to be found such questions as the nature of the obligation to truth in advertising and to disclosure of risks to consumer health and safety. Here, too, are questions about the openness of the market system, fair competition, and just restraint in the use of concentrated economic power.

A fourth arena of work-world concern lies in the relation of the institution to the social and material environment. Is there concern to conserve depletable resources, because future generations are also our "neighbors"? Is there concern to avoid polluting air and water and soil, to enhance the quality of life in the local community where the organization operates?

Finally, we in work encounter matters of regulatory and statutory law. The manager and tradesperson confront regulations about building codes, safety standards, patent rights, labeling, and fair trade practices. Every wage earner and professional meets government through income tax reporting. In a democratic society, obedience to the spirit of laws and regulations is usually a mark of moral maturity and an act of responsible social participation. Civil disobedience on moral grounds is the rare exception that proves this rule. In obeying the law, we acknowledge the moral claims of the wider society on us, as formulated through the political process.

A Framework for Work-World Counsel

In pastoral conversation and teaching that are work related, the minister will find some help in turning again to Lawrence Kohlberg's developmental theories. First, Kohlberg reminds us of the pedagogical principle that growth takes place through interacting with others, and through having one's own standards and assumptions questioned. Leon Festinger researched what he called "cognitive dissonance," which happens when two elements of knowledge do not fit together, and a person is forced by the internal desire for consonance to think through the disjunction (Festinger, 1957). Moral growth is analogous. In adults, it does not come naturally, as romantic assumptions would have it, nor, on the other hand, does it come through being coerced by others to conform to moral rules. In the workplace, as in family life, someone needs often to challenge accepted standards, raise questions, blow the whistle, propose alternatives. The effective introduction of "dissonance" is not coercive or cynical, but constructive and reflective.

Second, and this is the heart of Kohlberg's system, moral development generally follows a sequence of stages. These stages, referred to in chapter 6, can be described in thumbnail fashion with the following excerpt from Kohlberg (1981, p. 19), in which he cites the "motive given for rule obedience or moral action" at each of the stages. (I add in parentheses the designated name for the stage.)

1. (The Punishment and Obedience Orientation) Obey rules to avoid punishment.
2. (The Instrumental Relativist Orientation) Conform to obtain rewards, have favors returned, and so on.
3. (The Interpersonal Concordance or "Good Boy-Nice Girl" Orientation) Conform to avoid disapproval and dislike by others.
4. (Society Maintaining Orientation) Conform to avoid censure by legitimate authorities and resultant guilt.
5. (The Social Contract Orientation) Conform to maintain the respect of the impartial spectator judging in terms of community welfare.
6. (The Universal Ethical Principle Orientation) Conform to avoid self-condemnation.

The importance of the stages for the moral counselor lies in the following assertion: Moral counsel or teaching will be most effective if it proposes a move of one stage at a time. Citing research by James Rest, Kohlberg argues that "Students prefer the highest stage of reasoning they comprehend but . . . they do not comprehend more than one stage above their own" (1981, p. 27).

This principle provides us guidance for moral coaching. In speaking of the gap between the work-world and the clergy, I cited our religious propensity for global moral exhortation. That leads us too often to miss the mark in close-up, one-on-one, or small group moral conversation about actual ethical quandaries. Kohlberg's assertion will help us. Instead of offering a global stage 6 maxim against the stage 3 or 4 level of a parishioner, we would do better with a less idealistic proposal. With Marty Sams, then, we do better by dropping the idealistic Bible interpretation and concentrating on the immediate dilemmas of the work-world conflict he is experiencing. We bracket for the moment any grandiose defense of or attack on the nature of the profit-motive. We say "Give us an idea of the bind," and let Marty talk about the way he has had to pay an employee less than she was worth, or how he was "obliged" by the rules of the game to destroy a competitor whose business was already shaky. In the study group, then, Marty Sams begins to integrate his description into a moral system—the relative importance of his firm's survival and the wages for the secretary, for example, or some other options in relating to the competitor.

Consider another case. An employer in a small family firm is thinking over the possibility of hiring for the first time a minority secretary. He resists the idea in stage 3 thought (avoiding disapproval by others) and cites the objections of other secretaries. It is not difficult to move into "stage four" thinking (law and order), hiring her "to avoid censure by legitimate authorities." Even discussion in terms of the "social contract orientation," stage 5 (fairness, "to maintain the respect of the impartial spectator"), will more likely move the employer farther than speaking in stage 6 terms (doing good to all, Kohlberg's "universal ethical principle" orientation).

One business ethics professor, Edward Conry, follows this approach explicitly as he describes a conversation between a nun and a parishioner. I have adapted the following from an unpublished manuscript of his.[1] As revealed in the parenthetical commentaries, Conry stresses the need for definite assessment of comments in light of Kohlberg's moral stages:

> KIM: So I'm not going to fire her. While she's our slowest assembler, I've already let 3 people go in the

---

1. Unpublished ms., 1985, Ed Conry, with Richard Vanasse.

last 6 months and I'm afraid it'll look like I can't pick good employees if I let her go too. (A statement at stage 3.)

SR. JOANNE: What happens if you get that reputation?

KIM: Then my boss would make those decisions, and he's a bigot. We'd have an all white, all male workforce in 2 years. (A statement at stage 4 or 5.)

SR. JOANNE: So your concern is that minorities receive fair treatment?

KIM: Sure. Besides, if my boss does the hiring, there'll be even more turnover; we won't meet our quota; and I'll lose out on the year-end bonus. (A statement at stage 3 or 4.)

SR. JOANNE: Which concerns you the most, Kim—the injury to minorities or the unfair impact on you?

KIM: It's those black guys who want jobs but can't get them. That really gets to me. I remember when my father couldn't get work because we're Catholic. I think we should apply the same hiring standards fairly to everyone. (A stage 5 motive statement.)

SR. JOANNE: I can understand how you feel. I'm glad you're so concerned for other people. There ought to be more people like you. (A gesture of moral empathy and reinforcement.)

We can note even in this brief segment the different levels at which a person is likely to respond to moral questions. As I said earlier, Carol Gilligan (1982) criticizes Kohlberg for enforcing a linear, "masculine" kind of moral development on his data, whereas there are other styles of moral growth, especially in women. However, keeping that criticism in mind to allow for other styles of work-world ethical discussion, the Kohlberg schema remains helpful.

The Impossible Possibility

For the minister, there is something unnerving in a strategy that suggests pulling back from New Testament idealism, as we proposed in referring to the study group and Marty Sams. Clergy do not readily talk in stage 4 terms when stage 6 is at hand. We are left wondering about what Reinhold Niebuhr called "the relevance of an impossible ethical ideal" (1935). Niebuhr holds on to the tension in prophetic religion, rather than relieve it in either of the two directions of disintegration he sees in religious history. "The one inclines to deny the relevance of the ideal of love to the ordinary problems of existence. . . . The other tries to prove the relevance of the religious ideal . . . by reducing it to conformity to the prudential rules of conduct" (p. 104).

For Niebuhr, the finite and self-interested human spirit will never attain perfection, and to think otherwise opens the gates of moralism and religious fanaticism. But the ideal is not an intolerable burden, despite what critics like Freud have argued, because faith knows the way of contrition. "Prophetic religion has resources for relaxing moral tension as well as for creating it" (p. 117). The redemptive activity of God balances the judging, and sinners are ascribed righteousness in the grace of God we know in Christ. That means freedom for continued moral effort, and the ideal, far from being an oppressive burden, is a gift of guidance.

In our terms, the ideal remains relevant to point out the direction of moral growth. The means will most likely be by way of incremental steps, without trying a longer leap toward perfection. That attempt creates the gap, and it fails. The "best" becomes bad for the good.

Pastoral Strategies in Work-World Ministries

We close this chapter with a number of strategies for the pastor in relation to the work-world. The background of these suggestions is the understanding that every employed Christian is called to morally reflective service in the occupational world. For most people, that is the primary arena of "lay ministry," for it consumes most of their energy and time. This kind of assumption can be expanded among the core leadership of a congregation once it becomes the pastor's mindset and is reinforced by consistent language in teaching and pastoral conversation. Many within the core leadership of a church already conceive of all their life, work-world included, as involved in Christian serving, Christian ministering.

1. Make work-world topics a regular part of preaching, teaching, and pastoral conversation. The pastor's record cards on families should always note breadwinners' vocation and workplace. Occupational illustrations in preaching should take their place alongside those from family life and notes on volunteer activity in the community. The goal is a richer consciousness of work as a locus of moral struggle and moral envisioning.

2. Remember the counselor-coach perspective. The expert in each field is the person deeply involved, not the outsider. The goal is the lay person's growth as a moral actor in the field. The minister is resource, instigator, and midwife for growth, not moral arbiter for right and wrong, sector by sector in the occupational world.

3. Read current materials pertinent to the demography of the congregation. In a blue collar parish, the pastor should subscribe to a trade union house organ. A rural pastor should take at least one farm magazine. In a university community a pastor may read the *Chronicle of Higher Education,* and in a business-oriented community one or more of the better business magazines. This kind of reading will facilitate pastoral conversation around work-related issues and feed the illustration file that is necessary for good teaching and preaching of the sort suggested in #1.

4. Keep the church alive as a public forum. Fellowship activities like men's and women's organizations, or couples clubs, may be stimulated with discussions on work-world issues, going well beyond the problems of family and community life. It is a legitimate part of mission for a church to invest staff time in meetings of this sort. Downtown urban churches often provide programming for business and professional people as a way of fostering the moral mission in the workplace.

5. Spawn as many work-sector interest groups as possible. Ideally, every professional and trade organization should constitute a self-critical agency for chipping away at moral problems in its own sector. Few do. Therefore,

conscientious lay men and women need to form their own support and dialogue groups. The minister can help, by convening groups according to occupational category, by helping people connect with one another, and by suggesting format for early meetings.

A young minister in an upstate New York farming community convened a team of parishioners for regular study over a period of three years. They produced a mimeographed volume of agribusiness ethics, concerning themselves with such issues as conservation, overseas hunger, farm implement sales pressures, and the ethical rationale of national policies. This is the minister's broker role again, helping people make connections, a role enhanced in this case by catalytic encouragement of moral reflection. Some clergy specialize, as labor priests, or as chaplains to fire or police departments; or they join civic clubs and meet weekly with a cross section of the business community, not merely for enjoyment, but with missional intent.

We can hold in mind two kinds of "maps" of society in relation to the church. On one, the ordinary kind, we mark out locations of church buildings by geographic neighborhoods. On the other, a map drawn by work sectors, we can imagine ecclesiolae, or minichurches, in each sector. Their fourfold purpose is not unlike that of churches on the first map—in prayer to celebrate the good and confess the wrong in a given arena of life, in fellowship to sustain their members in time of stress, in critical reflection to examine the moral quality of communal life, and with vision to organize for change.

6. Take pastoral care into the workplace. Pastoral visitation in homes has a long and important history. Less so, visitation at work. Yet we have the option of dropping by at offices, classrooms, commercial establishments, and even the manufacturing shopfloor for most working parishioners. That kind of visitation helps us know far better one aspect of our parishioners' lives. It symbolically reinforces the awareness that the church is wherever the people are. And it enhances the possibility of pastoral conversation pertaining to the work-world. In pursuing these goals, a number of suburban

pastors commute as often as once a week to meet with parishioners in the central cities where they work.

7. Heighten the awareness of work-world ethics with special conferences. One suburban congregation sponsored a well-publicized day-long convocation, drawing leadership from their own members for the most part, on issues of business ethics. The pastor coached the planning team, but he took a backseat during the day itself. The congregation and those attending were all nudged into a deeper awareness of morality in the occupational sector of their lives. Another similar conference was convened by an ad hoc committee of clergy and business educators from two nearby colleges. A wide number of Catholic parishes and area meetings have studied the Catholic bishops' pastoral letter on the American economy (N.C.C.B., 1986).

The Center for the Ministry of the Laity of Andover Newton Theological School has designed a day-long workshop format that serves to help lay people from any walk of life conceive of their own ministries in the work-world.[2] Participants share their self-understanding, across occupational lines, in ways that send them all back to work with clearer vision and greater perseverance in the arduous task of chipping away at ethics in the workplace.

---

2. The Center's address is 210 Herrick Road, Newton Center, MA 02159.

CHAPTER NINE

Moral Counsel in Medical Crisis

BOOKS, ARTICLES, AND TELEVISION PIECES
devoted to medical ethics are now legion. Their number
shows how much the progress of medical science has
intensified old ethical issues and plentifully spawned new
ones. Some of today's medical issues could barely have been
imagined by the best science fiction writers of a generation
ago. How long should a comatose person be sustained with
artificial respiration and feeding, when higher brain
functions are irreversibly gone? Who should have parental
rights when a surrogate mother changes her mind and
wants to keep the child already growing in her womb? Shall
every newborn, no matter how vegetative, deformed, and
brain damaged, be kept alive if it can be with medical
intervention? How much shall we intervene in human
genetic structure, the way we now do with animals to create
better chickens and cattle? How shall we decide which
eligible and critical patient will receive an available kidney
or heart for transplant? The questions go on and on.

Our pastoral work intersects with moral questions in
medical crises on three planes. In speaking of the
work-world, we have already alluded to one. We serve
medical personnel in the congregation, people whose work
is now permeated by new moral burdens and ambiguities.
They need pastors who have a sense of their burdens even

when those problems are not brought up in conversation. They need ministers to hold up their hands when they are weary, to help them sustain sensitivity to moral questions in the midst of both crisis and routine, to prevent moral burnout. Medical people can be caught between financial needs to economize and pressures for ambiguous, high-cost treatments that might be better. (The current cost-control strategy, involving diagnosis-related groups or DRG's, increases hospitals' economic incentives, and therefore the pressure, to discharge patients as early as possible.) Physicians are caught between the threat of malpractice litigation and the inevitable risks of crisis medicine, where human error can mean handicap or even death. (Obstetrical liability and malpractice insurance is so expensive in some areas that no one is left to deliver babies!)

Another plane of ethical concern involves far more people—potentially everyone in the parish—and this chapter deals primarily with that concern. People can be overwhelmed when, in their own lives or the lives of those near them, they confront unanticipated medical dilemmas. At such a time, they often turn to their clergy for support and counsel.

A third plane of involvement is more general—the church's task of helping enhance the public's moral wisdom and the cogency of public policy around medical concerns.

Because the moral issues in medicine are so broad-ranging, we must define our particular arena of discussion. We are not focusing on the discipline of medical ethics. That is not our purpose. Medical ethics is an enormously complex field of inquiry. Participants in it include medical personnel, lawyers, ethicists of diverse backgrounds, public officials, patients, and researchers. The good pastor must be aware of the field, even if no expert. But we are not studying medical ethics. We are reflecting on the minister's task, and that from a particular point of view, the moral counselor's.

Patient Autonomy

Throughout this study, we have argued that the minister's role is to encourage reflective and conscientious moral integrity rather than to enunciate behavioral rules. To begin, therefore, in medical matters, the moral counselor stresses patient autonomy. This concern plays a significant role in current discussions of medical ethics. Nurses' groups and hospitals draw up statements of patients' rights. Governmental commissions promulgate regulations on informed consent. More than ever before, physicians share with patients information about the risks involved in surgery and medication. The clergy can only applaud these trends.

We have two major roles as moral counselors. Both undergird autonomy. As pastors, we hope to be midwives of virtue, encouraging its birth and growth in our parishioners and others. And as educators, we teach moral principle and moral reasoning as we are able. Teaching moral rules may help, when we are clear about them, but rules can hardly cover every circumstance; and right actions by rote, without conscience or love, have little moral standing. We place ourselves alongside our parishioners in medical crisis, consultants that we are, as they and their doctors make decisions.

For a good initial summary of what autonomy implies in the medical sector, we can turn to the American Hospital Association's statement of a patient's rights. Among its statements are these:

The patient has the right to obtain from his [sic] physician complete current information concerning his diagnosis, treatment, and prognosis in terms the patient can be reasonably expected to understand. When it is not medically advisable to give such information to the patient, the information should be made available to an appropriate person in his behalf. . . .

Where medically significant alternatives for care or treatment exist, . . . the patient has the right to such information.

The patient has the right to refuse treatment to the extent permitted by law and to be informed of the medical consequences of his action. . . .

The patient has the right to examine and receive an explanation of his bill regardless of source of payment. (AHA, 1985, pp. 78-79)

A more explicit statement is found in a similar document quoted by Tom Beauchamp and James Childress in their text on medical ethics. Here, a patient has a right "to informed participation in all decisions involving his health care program," and "to a clear, concise explanation of all proposed procedures in layman's terms, including the possibilities of any risk of mortality or serious side effects, problems related to recuperation, and probability of success," and a right "to know the identity and professional status of all those providing service."

Spelling out these concerns this way reflects the fact that patients have encountered too much paternalism in medicine, and have found themselves befuddled and intimidated. Our moral role as clergy is to encourage their strength of self in the face of crisis. Standing alongside parishioner-patients, we may find ourselves their advocates.

One of the statements above points to a more particular concern of ours, encountered too often in pastoral practice: that time "when it is not medically advisable" to tell the patient. Truthfulness in the doctor-patient relationship is an issue that has long troubled physicians. Doubtless, there are times "when it is not medically advisable" to tell the patient of a bad prognosis, but they should be few and far between. When truth is suppressed, charades begin. Eroded trust and openness between family and patient— and nursing staff and patient, and pastor and patient—is a very high cost to pay for what is usually only a conjecture about medical gain. We as ministers teach, counsel, and pray for faith and courage in light of our mortality, with the end in view of what our medieval forebears called "a good death." Avoiding the issue at the end of life can sidetrack the patient's most important business at the time, and it can sidetrack the clergy's role of assistance in that business.

Moral autonomy requires truth. Beauchamp and Childress quote Samuel Johnson as they discuss the unpredictability of truth-telling's consequences:

I deny the lawfulness of telling a lie to a sick man for fear of alarming him. You have no business with consequences; you are to tell the truth. Besides, you are not sure what effects your telling him that he is in danger may have. It may bring his distemper to a crisis, and that may cure him. Of all lying, I have the greatest abhorrence of this, because I believe it has been frequently practised on myself. (p. 225)

Principled guidance of present process rather than uncertain consequentialist calculation is more consistent with our norms of respect for persons. We have stressed honest, open relationship between persons, and that goal has a general priority, standing against even benevolent deception. Sisela Bok (1978, p. 247) makes the same point as Johnson in arguing for disclosure by the physician—that people are more resilient than we expect, and that the long-term gains of trust in physician-patient relationship merit our deference. In our priestly capacities as "soul friends" or spiritual directors, a role that means we often speak with people about death and our human fears of it, we know this turf well. One of our contributions to medical personnel and patients, therefore, is encouraging less deception around the unfavorable prognosis. The religiously encouraged hospice movement has demonstrated how much is to be gained. Hospice care by medical staff and family members comes to be compassionate and tender in ways that are less likely in standard hospital settings.

Truth-telling need not be brutal. In the case of cancer, for example, it often does not need to destroy hope. Predictions can only be probabilities, because unexpected recoveries do occur. Surgeon Bernie Siegel, well known for encouraging health-giving attitudes in his cancer patients, disagrees with his colleagues about "false hope." "If nine out of ten people with a certain disease are expected to die of it, supposedly you're spreading 'false hope' unless you tell *all ten* they'll probably die. Instead I say each person could be the one who survives, because all hope is real in a patient's mind" (1986, p. 29, emphasis Siegel's).

Medical Ethics for the Pastor

Theological seminaries are now offering courses on medical ethics, and the Clinical Pastoral Education movement annually offers close-up experience of the medical environment to hundreds of seminarians. Nonetheless, it is appropriate here to add a few comments on the principles of medical ethics, before looking into some pastoral cases.

As in any other ethical field, medical ethics displays considerable diversity according to the kind of reasoning that is employed. Some ethicists are far more inclined to stress individual rights, others the social good. The former tend to be rule-oriented, deontological thinkers, while the latter more consequentialist, more utilitarian. To revert to the question above, for example, the first would stress the principle of veracity, the latter the importance of beneficent behavior toward the patient, not harming the patient unnecessarily by reporting bad news. These two different perspectives emerge as both patient-parishioners and medical personnel speak with us about health and moral concern. Helping a parishioner clarify his or her reasoning is part of our ministry.

We have already identified one of the basic principles around which medical ethics discussions swirl, that of autonomy. Another guideline—and here I am following the framework of Beauchamp and Childress—is that of nonmaleficence. These authors quote an ancient adage, *"Primum, non nocere,"* or, "First of all, do no harm." Nonmaleficence holds a stronger claim on us than does doing good. We must certainly avoid injuring a pedestrian even if we do not go the extra bit and stop, good Samaritan fashion, to assist an injured man along the road. Failure in the first instance earns far greater penalty than in the second. In medical treatment, we undertake the risk of harm through surgery or medication only when greater harm of suffering will result from our inaction or when there are almost certain probabilities of benefit. Trusting the physician not to harm us is an extremely important part of the doctor-patient relationship. This fact in itself accounts in no small way for the medical resistance to euthanasia, let alone other reasoning. The ancient Hippocratic tradition stresses this principle: "I will keep [the sick] from harm and injustice. I will neither give a deadly drug to anybody if asked for it, nor will I make a suggestion to this effect. Similarly I will not give to a woman an abortive remedy." Given that rule, one can easily sense the seriousness of a doctor's decision to take from a living person a donor kidney, even for a near relative of the donor.

A third principle is the complement to nonmaleficence—beneficence. As stated, this can be regarded as a weaker duty than avoiding harm. In spite of the *moral* claims, "A physician has no legal duty to stop at the scene of an automobile accident or to answer affirmatively when the manager of a restaurant or theater asks 'Is there a doctor in the house?' " (Beauchamp and Childress, 1983, p. 157). Physicians do not take fifty-fifty risks between doing good and doing harm. When risks are involved, as they often are, the calculations of cost and benefit must lean preponderantly toward the positive side before proceeding. To note the difficulty of these calculations, however, I will cite but one of the cases from Beauchamp and Childress, that of a

premature infant born by caesarean section after a 34-week gestation period. At birth the baby was "blue, limp, had no reflexes, and a very slow heart rate"—and also had excessive fluid and an enlarged liver and spleen. The parents wanted the child very much, and intense resuscitation measures were initiated. At 14 minutes of age the child was doing poorly and had no spontaneous activity. The doctors feared that "there is an extremely high risk" that a retarded baby (at best) would result from further medical efforts. Physicians and nurses expressed strong differences of opinion as to whether resuscitation efforts should continue, at least if the baby stopped breathing. (p. 165)

In a situation like this, what kind of intervention is doing the greater good and for whom? Opinions are bound to differ, depending not only on medical information but also on ethical style and on theological belief.

We have spoken of paternalism. As an issue, paternalism is the flip side of autonomy. Beneficence raises the issue, Do we do good against a person's own preferences, against autonomy? Should we legislate the use of seatbelts by people who prefer not to use them, or is this an unwarranted intrusion against self-direction? The Jehovah's Witnesses as a matter of faith refuse blood transfusions. Medical people, under obligations of beneficence, have asked courts for permission to save lives by ordering transfusions. The courts have done so for minor children, but usually not for adults, on grounds of patient autonomy. A person may refuse medical treatment, and beneficence should not override.

Fourth, medical ethics has to deal with justice. What is the fair way to distribute limited resources—of health-care money, of organs for transplant, of medical personnel? Do we invest for prevention or cure? Should a given sum be spent "on one young adult needing a heart transplant? On two or three children in need of kidney transplants? On a hundred children suffering from malnutrition? On 5,000 persons in a genetic-screening program or 20,000 in need of inoculations?" (Nelson and Rohricht, 1984, p. 193). We now believe at least minimal food and clothing are a right of everyone, although we don't always succeed in living out that belief. How much health care is a social entitlement, the right of everyone? (Legally, it now includes dialysis, an expensive commitment of federal dollars.) And what health care items are to be left to freemarket choices and ability to pay?

Every pastor ought to be familiar with at least one good book on pastoral care of the sick and one on medical ethics. We are not arguing that every pastor possess professional medical ethics expertise, but that he or she be ready for informed participation as theologian and counselor with parishioners, and with medical and community groups in face of medical crisis.

Cases

1. Two of Mark Jones' parishioners, Jack and Sarah Kline, have turned forty. They were married in their late thirties, by Mark, at St. Andrew's altar. Unfortunately, they seemed unable to have children. Now, however, Sarah is pregnant. The couple is delighted, but Sarah's doctor

recommends amniocentesis because her age and family history put her pregnancy at risk. Jack and Sarah are devastated to receive the report—the fetus is genetically impaired with Down syndrome. Their child will be mildly or severely retarded, they cannot tell which. Sarah calls Mark, in tears. What should she do?

Mark's first task is to listen and to comfort, of course. What, beyond that, is his role? Does he try to justify God, when Jack says, "Why does this happen to us?" Does he discuss abortion? Does he teach a minicourse on medical ethics? Does he tell stories about other parents in similar circumstances?

Mark has certain resources to offer. He is a good counselor and can feel with moving empathy the deep despair in Sarah. He is sensitive to the spiritual struggle in Sarah and Jack—their wonderment at new life growing, and their fear for the future. As an experienced pastor, Mark knows a broker role; he can put the Klines in touch with families with Down syndrome children. He knows St. Andrew's people will gather round the Klines in support, if and when the need arises.

Mark has also thought long and hard about abortion. He has identified for himself what he sees as legitimate opposition to it by "conservatives" and what he sees as immoral legalisms on that same conservative side of the abortion debate. He rubs professional shoulders with a pastor who would not in conscience participate with a couple in any decision for abortion. He has reviewed both the serious-minded concern and what he thinks of as trivial shallowness found among the various advocates of a more liberal position. Mark is particularly aware of a sexist dimension to the abortion debate. He resents the fact that for centuries, a male-dominated society, with punitive, patriarchal overtones, and without inviting women into the debate, rationalized positions that affect women profoundly. He knows the frequent and tragic necessity of weighing conflicting goods, and the moral dangers of making absolute the value, in this case, of either fetal life or Sarah and Jack's hopes and fears. Therefore, he can truly hear them as Jack and Sarah one moment say, "Let's let this one go and try again," and the next, "This is a human life." Mark is the moral counselor, not the judge.

For himself, Mark opposes most abortion, not as "murder," but as the interruption of a developing, although still only potential, human personal life. He allows for times when other moral claims may take precedence. He has preached and taught about his position and his reasons for it.

In working with the Klines, Mark is prepared to do several things. Mark is able to share his opinions with Sarah and Jack without dogmatism, affirming their freedom to think things through in a different way. Mark will be patient, not rushing Sarah and Jack to a premature decision, in spite of the urgency. He will be prepared for extended counseling after the decision. He will be there with the Klines and their feelings of guilt in the event of an abortion, or with comfort and support should they respect the fetus in its evolution toward full human life, and should their child have serious problems.

Mark will not play God, trying to take the painful decision out of their hands, because autonomy holds a high value in his strategy of moral counsel.

2. For five years, Rachel Marquand, priest, has been visiting a parishioner, Irene Small, in an edge-of-town nursing home. Irene has been bright and cheerful most of the time, but now, at the age of eighty-nine, she is declining. Her pain is growing more intense; she has a terminal cancer and hasn't long to live. Her family is heavily burdened by the nursing home bills, and Irene wants to die. She now refuses to take food.

Today we encounter the "want to die" situation more and more frequently, since people are living longer. In the event of terminal illness, parishioners often want to exert some control over the manner and timing of their deaths. Great as is the mystery surrounding life and death, submissive fatalism is not the best word about terminal illness. The natural course of things is not to be equated with God's intentional will. In a sense, all medicine is intervention against the "natural course of things." God's will is rather the well-being of the person. In the Netherlands, in terminal cases with unrelievable pain, euthanasia is openly allowed when patients ask for medical help in dying. In this country, cases of "mercy killing" sometimes reach the courts, but usually they take place sub rosa. Nonetheless, the demand will increase, and clergy will find parishioners wanting to talk over the morality of self-chosen death.

We teach with several convictions that arise from Christian faith. (1) We believe life is given as a sacred trust, and it is not to be measured ultimately by its usefulness, its ease, its length, even its moral virtue. If it fails in any or all of these respects, it is not to be dismissed as worthless. (2) Life is a calling, and we are to find our way in it as such. At one stage or another, our calling may be little more than faithfully and trustfully coping with seemingly impossible suffering and disability. (3) Medicine makes it possible to prolong our dying, and this is legitimately distinguished from prolonging our living. To prolong dying may be to inflict unwanted suffering on patients and others alike, to no principled moral purpose. The way doctors and patients and moral counselors deal with dying is not necessarily a matter for the courts at all.

Rachel's work with Irene Small can take guidance from all three of these convictions. Each day that Irene is able to live, Irene may take comfort in her faithfulness. It is a testimony to the gift of life. Taking food can be an act of courage. If Irene instead interprets her suffering as nothing but an untimely extension of her dying, Rachel may choose to minister in a different vein. Instead of praying for strength, she will find herself praying with Irene for peace. She will want to hear confession, and to turn more toward the family in preparation for death. Irene is to be respected in her choice, so long as Rachel has not failed to offer her also the respect of shared conviction, and even argument, along the lines just listed.

An American Hospital Association report describes a case of self-chosen termination of dialysis by a forty-year-old diabetic, a choosing of death. The woman did not want to face the reduced quality of life that would result from a necessary amputation of both legs below the knee. She had been on dialysis nine years. A psychiatrist judged her to be free of clinical depression, able to make her own decision. The hospital staff and the patient's physician "outlined a plan of care for Mrs. D., which included termination of dialysis with the expectation of subsequent coma and death. A plan was outlined, whereby the staff would maintain Mrs. D.'s comfort throughout this final ordeal" (AHA, 1985, p. 63).

A pastor working with Mrs. D. and her doctor would need to weigh the prognosis after a surgical amputation. Was it likely to add years to life, or to prolong dying? Mrs. D.'s fears about losing independence are justified, but mutual dependence in the human community is a Christian understanding of life that should be vigorously stressed as well. God values Mrs. D.'s living, and others do. Every one of us is in many ways dependent on human neighbors. This we would attempt to help Mrs. D. deeply comprehend. It is a fourth perspective, to be added to the three principles listed for Irene Small and Rachel. Nonetheless, Mrs. D. has the right, ultimately, to will her death rather than to succumb to paternalistic coercion from either the medical system or the religious.

3. Ken Fowler, a sixty-year-old biochemist, has stomach cancer, with extensive metastatic involvement of the lymph system and other organs, discovered during stomach surgery. Radiation and chemotherapies are only palliative, and the situation is explained to Ken. As a scientist, he fully understands the situation. Now the onset of lung involvements and heart failure triggers frenetic staff efforts to sustain his life, but Ken insists that he is not to be resuscitated the next time. Twice the hospital staff ignores his request, and Ken turns to his pastor for moral support.

A similar case is found in Beauchamp and Childress. Four times a hospital's emergency staff revived a man, a physician, whose pain and negative prognosis had prompted him earlier to say, in writing, that he did not want to be resuscitated in the event of heart failure.

The medical mindset does battle with death. It is

well-armed for the struggle. Medical reflexes follow that mindset. Pastoral concerns in Ken's situation are different. The pastor stands on the side of the patient, whose rights are being violated. Were the pastor the chaplain, there would be more leverage available. The minister, from the community, is a guest on medical turf. He or she, however, has influence with the family if there is one, and influence with the religious chaplaincy if there is one. By spending time with the patient, the minister earns voice with the medical staff as well.

4. To suggest yet another kind of situation, I quote from James Nelson and Joanne Smith Rohricht (pp. 176-77):

Two years after the removal of one cancerous breast, Ruth Blake developed serious kidney disease. One kidney was removed for malignancy. A year later the other kidney became dysfunctional and was removed, but no cancer was found. Kept on dialysis, the patient raised the question of a transplant. While her brother was willing, indeed anxious, to donate a kidney to Ms. Blake, the medical staff were not eager to accept his offer. They knew that posttransplant patients receiving those drugs (immunosuppressives) which combat the body's attempt to reject the new organ are statistically more likely to develop malignancies than is the normal person. And Ms. Blake's malignancy history was not good. On the other hand, a cadaver kidney would not offer her as great a chance for success as one from her brother.

As in many cases, we find here such an overriding importance in medical knowledge and research that we almost wonder how the patient or the patient's pastor has any say in the matter at all. If Ruth's prognosis is bad, her brother is likely to have taken a foolish risk should his proposal be accepted. If the prognosis is good, he may want to proceed. In these cases the lay person needs to remember both that we need to obtain the best information available, but that we do not necessarily defer to the advice given us by people from the technical disciplines. This decision, like many, should include both technical information and moral judgment.

The Christian patient and family member may have a different bias from that of medical personnel as such. The persons who make up the medical system are conditioned against accepting risks to physical and mental health. This is their proper role, so long as, in the hard cases, there is also concern for the care of the patient as person. In Ruth's case, her brother, having heard the warnings, may yet as a Christian choose to proceed with the risks. In the back of his mind are the assurances that God cares for him and for his sister, in life or death. He knows too that the disciple may lay down life for good ends, and that cost-benefit analysis is not the last word in love and care for a near neighbor.

Broader Leadership

Besides offering pastoral care and counsel at times of crisis, the pastor takes on a more general leadership role vis-à-vis health and medicine. He or she can help prepare families for medical crisis. It will help if the minister has already led the congregation to reflect on biomedical issues.

Mark Jones has sat with a family, for example, while a surgeon was trying to save the life of their son, the victim of a motorcycle accident. The doctor warned them there was little hope. How difficult it was, during those crucial hours, and after the bad news came, to raise the possibility of donating organs for transplant. Mark wished he had discussed the issue in preaching, teaching, and the church's newsletter in advance of this painful time. Mark was convinced that giving such permission is an important and lifesaving act of Christian beneficence. But he also realized a family may withhold permission, given the trauma of grief, without such advance preparation. Mark realized he had never spoken up, as he might have in his state, urging people to sign up on their driver's licenses for organ donation.

Increasingly, Mark has helped people plan ahead for the problem of prolonged dying. He has suggested a brief "living will" that directs families and medical personnel what to do in the event a person loses competence to make medical decisions for himself or herself. "I ask that I be allowed to die and not be kept alive indefinitely by artificial means or heroic measures. I am not asking that my life be directly taken, but that my dying be not unreasonably prolonged if my condition is hopeless, my deterioration irreversible, and the maintenance of my life an overwhelming responsibility for my family or an unfair monopoly of medical resources."

The living will is a morally reasoned affirmation. The one-page document Mark uses begins, "I, (N), as a Christian, believe that 'whether we live or whether we die, we are the Lord's (Romans 14:8).' If death is certain, so is the faithfulness of God in death as in life. With this high hope to sustain me, I wish to be as responsible in dying as in living."[1] The form provides space for reaffirmations at later dates. The living will is helpful for discussions with families and physicians, and for church study groups as well.

When a parish family raises questions arising from a medical dilemma, the minister who knows some of the hospital staff and doctors of the community holds a great advantage. He or she is then able, through conversation with the medical people, to corroborate what a family in stress thinks they have been told. Medical information cannot be given to strangers; but professional colleagues may share it. More and more hospitals see the chaplain as part of the healing team, and, by extension, the local clergy, if they have built up the necessary interprofessional trust.

Broader moral leadership related to medicine may also involve a pastor in public advocacy for a better distribution of our health-care dollars. The pastor discovers families who fall into the cracks in our present health-care system, lavish as that system is in helping some. These families are receiving little or no care because they haven't the money or the insurance. Or they may have woefully mortgaged their future in paying bills that would have been covered for most families. The moral imperatives of distributive justice demand attention to these cracks in the system. This public

---

1. New Samaritan Communications Corporation, 1975, distributed by Eden Publishing House.

role for the moral counselor, however, is taken up in the next chapter.

Finally, some local clergy may be asked to serve on hospital ethics committees. Large urban hospitals will use in-house clergy, medical school chaplains, or theologian-ethicists for these committees, but a smaller community may not have such specialists available. If so invited, a community or clergy representative will be scrupulous about confidentiality, serious but not stubborn about unusual moral positions of his or her particular religious tradition, and respectful of medical learning while recognizing that moral matters are everyone's concern, not just the physician's and the nurse's. (From a strictly medical point of view, an abortion is a "procedure"; the right or wrong of it involves more than medicine.) The minister who accepts a place on a hospital ethics committee is committed to serious study and reflection; if time for that is not available, the invitation should be declined.

In sum, the minister offers a moral resource to the persons who work in medicine and to families and patients in medical crisis. That resource offers empathic support and the strength of a moral tradition. Both are likely to be needed in the agonizing decisions that are required in current health-care experience.

CHAPTER TEN

Moral Counsel
in the Public Square

RICHARD JOHN NEUHAUS CALLED HIS RECENT
book "about religious politics and political religion" (p. vii)
The Naked Public Square. The title summed up his chief
concerns. The public arena has been stripped of the
common moral assumptions that once clothed our common
life, says Neuhaus. To change the metaphor, out of the
public arena, we inhabit a morally vacant house, and the
concern is that a whole clan of demons may now enter
(Matt. 12:43-45).

Neuhaus argues that we have moved from championing a
secular state to championing a secular society. But the two
are not the same. "Democracy is not to be equated with a
laissez faire morality in which 'anything goes'." Neuhaus
emphasizes the essentially religious foundation of democracy. "First, democratic government is premised upon the
acknowledgment of transcendent truth to which the
political order is held accountable. Second, democracy
assumes the lively interaction among people who are acting
from values that are, in most instances, grounded in specific
religious belief" (p. 120). Therefore, "we need to look for
quite unprecedented ways of relating politics and religion,"
to "devise forms for that interaction which can revive rather
than destroy the liberal democracy that is required by a
society that would be pluralistic and free" (p. 9).

This chapter deals with the pastor's relation to the public square. The moral counselor cannot ignore the social structures that profoundly shape human life, both in our own country and even throughout our global village.

This dimension of our concerns enormously complicates the force field. The norms and operative assumptions of society arise from many centers of initiative. Among these centers are political and governmental processes, educational institutions, the communications network, and a multitude of voluntary associations, families, and neighborhoods. Behind them all, shaping them as well as being shaped by them, are a people's most fundamental attitudes, their operative religious and quasireligious beliefs. And these attitudes and beliefs, of course, are our particular concern as clergy.

The ordained minister, whether wanting it or not, is a public figure, an "opinion maker." Our pastoral influence may seem slight enough with the fifty or five hundred directly addressed on a Sunday morning, let alone the wider community. But even the nightly newscasters do not participate in the lives of parishioners as we do, combining face-to-face pastoral history—around births, deaths, baptisms, weddings, and the crises of sickness and personal struggle—with the signs and symbols of God. The minister is positioned, no matter how much people explicitly disagree with his or her moral standpoints, to get under people's skin. He or she can represent conscience and cultural ideals for people. Like a pebble tossed into a placid pond, a pastor's conversations can start ripples that grow outward in the community beyond the faithful few.

I note all this for a simple reason. It further heightens the seriousness of ministry. We must be faithful stewards of our leadership role. Our influence, great or small, is to be used responsibly. It is not to be squandered on making the church into a country club. It is not to be invested in sustaining the status quo if that is corrupt or unjust. And it is not to be exploited for selfish or trivial ends.

Responsibility includes moral teaching and witness. If it does not, the gospel of God, the God of the biblical revelation, is being distorted. Another god is being proclaimed, not the Christian God who asks that justice and righteousness flow on earth like mighty rivers, and that the least among our brothers and sisters be cared for in their needs.

Our moral witness does not spring from grandiose ideas of making over the world. It springs from trying to be faithful to God. As John Yoder says in *The Politics of Jesus,* our model and leader Christ Jesus "gave up every handle on history" (p. 239).

Three common misunderstandings distort the public's understanding of religion in relation to society.

1. One misunderstanding is the idea that religion and politics don't mix. Both religion and politics deal with human values. Therefore they are bound to meet—and "mix." For good reason we Americans added to our Constitution a separation of sectarian, institutional religion from official governmental life. That is all we did. We set up a secular political process. But we did not ordain a secular or religionless society. The free exercise clause was sympathetic to religion, not hostile. "We are a religious people," said Justice Douglas (not himself a formal religious participant) in the 1952 Supreme Court decision on released public school time for religious instruction, *Zorach vs. Clauson.* It is to be expected that religious activity will continually impinge on and try to shape public policy.

2. Another misunderstanding is the idea that Christian faith is "personal," meaning individual and private, while politics is collective and public. On the contrary, both Old Testament and New Testament religion stress the social dimension of Godward faith. Narrowing religious concerns, focusing them overwhelmingly on the individual's emotive, "spiritual" God-relation, indispensable as this dimension to our faith may be, is a mistaken reading of the Christian text. Responsible teaching, preaching, and pastoral care must combine private piety with concern for the public weal, with the socially structured, "public" love of neighbor.

3. A third misunderstanding is similar to the second.

Social change, it is asserted, happens only when individuals change their behavior. If people one by one will get their hearts right with God, social policy will take care of itself. That view fails to understand the depth of our social nature as persons. Our evolution into thinking, feeling human persons is a social process. This is true to such an extent that the fact of the matter could almost (though not quite) be put the other way around. If the social environment—health care, food and housing, family upbringing, schooling, and the influence of the whole culture—were right, individual fulfillment, faith, and neighbor-love would take care of themselves. Both social milieu and private inner struggle shape a human life, but the two cannot finally be separated.

I am arguing, then, that Christ's command, "Tend my sheep," cannot mean for the conscientious pastor a narrow in-house preoccupation with the personal faith and private morality of parishioners alone. We tend God's flock by compassionate pastoral care combined with concern for the "public square," for the social and political ethic.

We have an enormous obligation to that value-hungry public square because of society's need for religious grounding and because of a faith that cares what happens to people. We of the religious community will not coercively dictate to public life. As Christians, we respect others. That is fundamental in our moral disposition. We are committed to love those with whom we disagree, and even our enemies. But the responsible church, on the basis of its moral concerns, cannot avoid passionate engagement with the civic world.

The obligation to the public square suggests certain elements in our ministry as moral counselors.

Elements of Style in Public Moral Witness

The moral counselor's participation in the public arena will make evident first of all a tone of confession—confession in both its religious senses. We speak in contrition, aware of our own sin and our own entanglement in the world's callousness, dullness, and cruelty. And we also confess our belief, on the basis of which we are committed to certain moral positions. Confession of the first sort prevents us from claiming power over others that could be abusive or repressive. It respects the other person, honors him or her, in keeping with the principle of autonomy. It diminishes violence of speech and action, making way for greater gentleness, even in the midst of strenuous disagreement. It opens the way for moral discourse instead of mere argument. Confession of the second sort provides coherence and grounding to our ethical assertions.

Second, our assertions and proposals in the public arena must respect reason. David Tracy calls for "public theology," theology that states religious truth-claims in a way that can be understood by those outside a particular religious tradition. Confessing belief does not require fideism. Faith seeks understanding; it attempts to share that understanding with others. This entails a search for common ground among people of differing perspectives. It means that in a discussion, two parties who may be at odds in some fairly fundamental assumptions nonetheless engage in a quest for truth. Failing to agree on what is true, they at least seek an accommodation to each other for the sake of the public order, justice, and compassion.

Neuhaus castigates Christian fundamentalists at this point, sympathetic as he is with their anxiety about the naked public square.

Fundamentalist leaders rail against secular humanists for creating what I have called the naked public square. In fact, fundamentalism is an indispensable collaborator in that creation. By separating public argument from private belief, by building a wall of strict separationism between faith and reason, fundamentalist religion ratifies and reinforces the conclusions of militant secularism.

(p. 37)

A final element of style ought to be humor. We do not take ourselves with such seriousness that we are blinded to the resources of grace in a situation—and the need for grace. In a sense the effective moral counselor is like a court jester. Sometimes to great moral purpose, the jester mocks those who take themselves too seriously. He entertains, sometimes with urgent double meanings. He lets in light from a source of intellect and wit that transcends the routine dimensions of business as usual.

These three elements will be more easily understood if we imagine an ideal participant and commentator in a public affairs television panel. Call her Mary Virtue. Mary has religious convictions and she is able and willing to share them. A person knows she is serious about her comments and the issues at hand. She is not simply churning out talk for talk's sake. Furthermore, her arguments are well reasoned. They reflect thought and unexaggerated fact as well as articulate religious faith and passion. Mary is prepared, therefore, to listen to counter argument, to concede countervailing possibilities, reasonably presented, and to understand ambiguities in issues of common concern. She does not try to overwhelm an opponent with extra volume, strident lecturing, or rude interruptions. And finally, Mary Virtue speaks with even more than faith-grounded exhortations and reasoned assertions. She can tell a story, joke and jest, and compliment an opponent. She can communicate respect while showing up the weakness or immorality in the argument being presented by an antagonist. She shares deep Christian moral reasoning and conviction, but she is neither pompous nor imperious in her moral pronouncements, and she is not dull.

If people of the church are to contribute much to moral discourse and behavior in the public square, they need to practice continually where it is easier (or ought to be!)—in the congregation. A serious-minded member of one church recently left it, explaining his reasons for going to a more conservative communion. "At coffee hour I could talk about our families, and about the Sunday school, and even about the Boston Red Sox, but never about the sermon. No one would talk theology with me, in church!" He was right, at least in his complaint. The church should be a community of moral reflection and discussion par excellence. From that base, clergy and laity should be adept at initiating and deepening morally serious discussion in the public square.

We look at the process of congregational development in chapter 11.

Myth-breaking by the Moral Counselor

One role of the moral counselor is to help people come to terms with moral realities. This is no easy task; it doesn't happen by simple explanation. The court jester points helpfully to one aspect of the task in doing this. The jester brings light from beyond the affairs at hand by means of parable and jest. He or she helps people do a moral double-take, to raise an eyebrow, to take a second and deeper look at operative ethical assumptions, puncturing myths and sundry "certainties." He engages in indirect communication, like that of Kierkegaard's parables and pseudonyms. Here are several American myths that from the Christian point of view, cry out for demolition.

Myth #1. "We're the best." Love of country needn't rest on superiority, much as the superpatriot argues that it does. We are one nation among others, and knowing the way God cherishes all people, the Christian dare not pretend to such primacy. Whether the arguments of "best" treat international trade, armaments, art, sport, or political systems, the assumptions that less than first place is unacceptable generate anxiety and hostility, not the world's well-being.

In the days when the Avis slogan was "We're only number two; we try harder," a young counterculture rebel at Kennedy Airport sported a large green button that said, "We're only number three, and we don't give a damn." I told the story once to a group of upwardly mobile suburbanites, on retreat, and in the question period one executive said he didn't understand. "If you're not trying to be number one," he said, "what's the purpose of living?"

One of the purposes of global education in school and church is an appreciation of other cultures. We grow able to understand the virtues of other cultures, and to see that people can prefer their own cultures to ours—an appalling idea to the narrow-minded. All this does not mean we cannot be profoundly grateful for most of our national heritage. A sense of loyalty and responsibility to one's own country's needs is a proper patriotism, and a virtue. It does not involve either a disdain for the self-interests of other nations or a compulsive conviction that "We're the best."

Myth #2. "Capitalism is the Christian way for economics." This myth mixes categories as badly as would the statement "Cubism is the Christian way for art," or "Organic farming is the Christian way for agriculture." There are moral virtues in free-market systems, but there are plenty of Christian socialists. All present-day economic systems are mixed, at any rate.

There are Christian and moral tests to be used with any economic system, our own included. As Christians we are concerned for the system's influence on people's spirit of cooperation and creativity, its treatment of the environment, its care for the handicapped and the poor, its social viability, its stability, its power to form new wealth, its "fit" with other values of a given culture, its openness and freedom for personal expression and personal autonomy. In short, Christian judgments must try to take account of far richer a skein of values than efficiency, productivity, and the money value of the Gross National Product. A given Christian community, in a given social situation, may favor and urge one economic form over others, but it is idolatrous to identify one or another as uniquely Christian. The church and its faith antedate capitalism by a dozen centuries.

Myth #3. "The enemy is evil; and we are noble." The Christian knows that nobility and evil exist on both sides of any of the world's curtains of enmity. The Christian also knows a provocative commandment: "Love your enemy." This injunction neither pretends there is no enemy, nor pretends that the enemy is a friend, or has no faults. It does mean we affirm and accept God's intention in sustaining the enemy in existence, and do not turn our principled opposition, if it must continue, into a crusade. Total war and slogans like "unconditional surrender" result when this myth stands unquestioned. So does untold suffering that might have been avoided.

Playwright Willy Holtzman has written a play, *Bovver Boys*, about tough, death-dealing urban street gangs in Scotland, among whom he worked in the '70s. After one public reading of the play, a member of the audience asked Holtzman about differences of social class or ethnicity among the warring factions. The playwright replied, "There was none. What struck me the most was how absolutely alike these boys were, and how *they have to invent their differences*—hair, dress, loyalties of turf. *Then they go to war over them.*"[1] His comment sums up one dark facet of our human condition.

Myth #4. "We earn, deserve, and own what we have; it's all ours." This patently false myth legitimates greed. All our wealth is drawn from God-given natural resources and from a complex social pool, a pool that is itself the beneficiary of centuries-long economic and technological developments by others. Our added expertise and labor is but slight, considering all that. In Christian terms, what we have is a gift, and we are but stewards. In paying taxes and giving to charity, we participate in the redistribution of wealth, which belongs to all. The ancient Hebrew designation of the jubilee year in Leviticus 25 and 27, whether it was ever practiced or not, reminds us of the claims of distributive justice, and that we hold wealth as merely temporary trustees of it.

A Congressman from Connecticut was reporting once on questions he encountered from constituents. "What do we of this little state have to do with the wheat farmers of Montana?" "Why should we who earn our own way pay to help families on welfare?" "I tell people," said the legislator, "that I thought we settled this kind of question in 1787. We decided we were one country, and later we fought a gruesome war to preserve that union." As Christians we go beyond even that nation-building rationale in our own doctrine of stewardship. Our wealth is not "all ours."

---

1. Emphasis mine.

For Instance

We turn now to suggestions for the kind of church witness that reaches into the public square. The goal in each case is to inject religiously grounded moral concern into social life beyond the private piety and individual moral striving of Christians. The goal is a stronger ethic in the public square.

First of all, in teaching and public witness we are to *preach the whole text*. By the whole text at this point I mean three things: The religious ground, the personal moral import, *and* the societal implications. It is hard to say which way we most often fail. Too often, certainly, we forget the third; we stop at personal implications of a text without looking to a wider horizon, without addressing the public square. But just as often, I believe, we offer exhortation to better personal morals or nobler public policy without deeply grounding it all in religious understanding. We start the "so what" sections of our sermons before rehearsing our Christian conversion, as it were. In addressing the world, we are to preach the whole text.

In 1987, at the funeral of William Casey, who was until his death the Director of the CIA, Bishop John McGann preached. He not only offered comfort and Christian hope to Casey's family and friends. He also pointed to the church's moral disagreements with Casey's stand on the way toward peace. He was widely criticized for injecting a moral note into a pastoral moment. Such a funeral, however, was a very public occasion, almost an occasion of state. Therefore it was not inappropriate for the "whole text" to have been expounded. It was an opportunity for moral discourse in the public square.

Week in and week out the events we sponsor are less dramatic than William Casey's funeral, but they are urgent too. In them we will expound both the personal and the public dimensions of our faith. On the personal plane, for example, love for neighbor means treating people we encounter without racial prejudice and discrimination. But neighbor-love also means legislation that shapes our public ethic, opening ways for the victims of discrimination to be accorded their due.

Fidelity and concern for family life mean cherishing the beloved, and disciplining one's lustful flirtations. But they also mean a public ethic and legislated policy that counteract facts like this one: In the year following desertion or divorce, the typical standard of living for the woman drops more than 70 percent and the man's goes up by more than 40![2] Pastoral concerns means advocacy for better child support laws to counteract the feminization of poverty. It means supporting welfare policies that encourage low-income fathers to be present rather than absent.

Reconciliation means interpersonal harmony, growing from reconciliation with God. But it means also the quest for disarmament and an end to demonizing all our political foes.

The first place for beginning public witness is to preach the whole text.

Second, the church may *create the deed to meet public need.* A few years ago, one dying mainline Protestant church, whose large building was located in a depressed area of one city, set up a soup kitchen several times a week at noon. In so doing, it came in contact with the people of the neighborhood in a new way.

As the autumn weather chilled, the church learned of the area's homeless, people with nowhere warm to spend the night. (The city's two "mission" shelters—a Salvation Army hostel and another evangelistic mission—had closed.) One old man froze to death in the city, under a porch.

The church opened its doors for overnight shelter, and that decision was a catalyst for much wider awareness and action for the homeless. Volunteers from suburban churches helped staff the shelter. The newspapers covered it. The mayor let the fire inspector look the other way for a season, as he cranked up city machinery to establish better and more legitimate space for a second winter. An ecumenical group of city-center churches took up the

---

2. *New Haven Register,* July 24, 1987, p. 13.

challenge and began planning for a permanent church-sponsored shelter. The entire city became aware of a human need. In the process the city reaffirmed an item in the public ethic, the right of everyone to shelter, whether able to pay or not. And through the same mission, it turned out, the original sponsoring church gained a new lease on life and mission.

Note the method in this public moral counsel: The pastor and congregation saw a need and reacted. The press picked up on the issue and informed the public. Other churches (the suburban volunteers, the city-center group) joined the action. The political structure responded.

Other and equally dramatic deeds to meet human need go farther afield. The sanctuary churches and the "overground railway" churches that help refugees in their legal transit through the States into Canada are meeting obvious needs. The "sister city" and sister congregation projects with Nicaraguan communities serve concrete human need in areas of obvious poverty. In serving the need, they subtly question the chauvinism that rejects the refugees or makes demons of the Sandinistas.

Third, the church will find ways to *offer a moral forum* for the public square. The church develops ways to use its resources of energy and influence to promote moral reflection in the wider community. I have mentioned the civic club format for business people. Many churches regularly invite Congress people and state legislators to address not only their in-house adult classes but publicly advertised forums. They sponsor other speakers and study groups—on medical ethics, Third World development, welfare or arms policy, East-West tensions.

Every community drifts toward morally lazy mindsets that need questioning by the court jester. The creative moral counselor and congregation will find ways to introduce the unpopular ideas—and the cognitive dissonance—to stimulate new thinking: the socialist Christian in a business-oriented community, the labor leader in a white collar town, the feminist theologian, the Christian artist, the gay rights advocate, the serious-minded proponent on each side of the abortion debate. Debate-discussions, with speakers on two sides of an issue, make it even clearer that the goal is not indoctrination but moral growth. The conferences on business ethics, reported in chapter 8, were forums for the public square.

Fourth, particularly in our time, to be interested in the public ethic means we must *think media*. Some have argued that television is the new religion of a post-Christian age. It is the world-defining substrate of value much as pervasive church life was in a former time. In the press and over television, people find rehearsed for them portrayals of a certain kind of world, and, by subtle implication, the way this world ought to be. Gregor Goethals (1981, pp. 33-85) calls T.V. the icon of our time, the image through which we interpret meaning, the place we "worship."

This line of reasoning is frightening, considering the mayhem and tawdriness of so much in the media "wasteland," but it is probably overdrawn. Human values and passions arise from other important sources—families, churches, and universities among them. But the argument is onto enough truth that we need to "think media" nonetheless.

The shelter project just described resulted in wider social ministry, in part because of the media. Forums will reach more people and better serve an always-evolving public ethic if they are well publicized in advance, through the media, and well reported after the event. Many a neighborhood event will reach but 30 to 300 in face-to-face engagement, and yet introduce a new idea—about health care, women's rights, disarmament, or whatever—to thousands through the day-after news item or a concurrent talk-show appearance by the out-of-town forum guest.

T.V. appearances and news items have nothing like the involvement of actual participation in a discussion meeting, but the seeds of reflection may be planted and nurtured nonetheless. If we think media, we will get more and more of the forum events themselves onto the under-used public access cable channels now available in every urban community. Again, cable listeners are not as involved as actual participants at the meeting, but they hear and see far more than they do in a second-hand news report of it.

Some church witness is legitimately aimed at public awareness more than anything else—and it depends heavily on the media because of it. Annually, on Good Friday, a large group carries the cross through "stations" at New England's U.S. submarine base. The goal is religious penitence and protest, an appropriate way to mark the day, with disarmament and peace the more specific goals. But public consciousness-raising is also in the minds of the marchers; the march is a graphic event for media portrayal and reporting.

Picketing a bank building to urge a stop to South African financial involvements is a way of speaking a word to passers-by. But picketers hope as well for media coverage—to nudge the thinking of the readers and viewers, and to exert wider public pressure on the bank.

A church-sponsored innercity action agency found the housing needs for homeless people growing desperate. So the agency helped homeless people organize a tent community on the town green. The protest was productive because of the media. It was a photogenic human interest story at the center of town, and through the media it reached thousands who never went past the city commons.

Good use of the media does not always take the time and organization that picketed or "media events" like the tent-out require. A carefully written letter to the editor can raise an issue for the moral concern of a community. The "readers write" sections of the papers are heavily read because of their personal interest, and the moral counselor can both write and encourage others. Exceptionally good writers (and even some mediocre ones) can often develop regular columns in the local press.

Finally, the moral counselor concerned for the public square will *think coalition.* Just as the personal counselor stands alongside the client in his or her struggle for growth, the parish church stands with, rather than aloof from, other community agencies. To be sure, the church holds a unique gift and responsibility in its life around Word and

Sacrament. As a human institution, however, it holds no monopoly on moral insight and virtue. Many agencies of a community mean well and do good. Participating *with* others is the course of choice for most enterprises aimed at a better public ethic. The church doesn't run the blood bank, but it helps the Red Cross do it. The League of Women Voters may run the debate, but the church will also publicize it. When the energies of a lay church leader are claimed for a year or two by the political party, or the school board, the pastor will encourage the person's work rather than fuss because it takes time from the church. Rightly understood, it is time well spent in ministry and mission.

One city's Women's Club had a "Department of International Relations," and for years cosponsored an annual class with a nearby church's midwinter school of religion. Religious concerns for peace are largely church-organized, but secular movements like Sane/Freeze, Bread for the World, Witness for Peace, Beyond War, or various student exchange programs may merit church encouragement.

Next, we examine the minister's moral counselor role as the congregation's leader.

CHAPTER ELEVEN

Coaching the Congregation Toward Moral Maturity

Basic elements of our moral counselor role have now emerged. First, we undertake pastoral care alert to a fundamental human need; namely, to base life upon a meaningful moral foundation. People need a goal for their lives larger than simply coping and solving personal problems. They need a nobler framework than the ultimately hollow one that urges us to seek in all things our own self-interest.

Second, we are aware that most of the norms of the counseling disciplines apply to the work of pastoral care. They are a legitimate part of the force field within which we undertake pastoral action. We respect autonomy, for example, and indeed affirm it as one of our own most basic values. One does one's own dying, Luther said, as one does one's own believing. Likewise, one's own moral action. Furthermore, as other counselors must, we too must begin with a parishioner where he or she is. Rapport and trust must grow. The pastor does not judge, in the sense of pretending to a higher moral status than the counselee.

Third, however, the minister is more than a mirror, more than a tool employed by a client for that client's psychological self-aggrandizement. By vocation, the pastor is minister of the church. He or she is engaged with the parishioner in a role that transcends "sustaining" support and even "healing." Seward Hiltner called this extra element the "guiding" function (1958). Clebsch and Jaekle (1964) find a fourth functional goal in ministry care, "reconciling"—not simply to God but also within the human community. We have discussed how the minister, in respecting the parishioner, will challenge and teach while counseling. He or she recognizes, in and around the present problem, the wider moral dimensions of the God-relation in which the parishioner stands and to which the religious community witnesses. As Gustafson put it (1982), the moral counselor offers an interrogatory role, raising questions to help the parishioner clarify ethical thinking for a choice of action.

Fourth, extending the "counselor" metaphor, we have gone on to say that the pastor is consultant to parishioners, encouraging them in active moral evaluation of their weekday worlds. This means that we cultivate a sense of the various ethical entanglements our parishioners must cope with—in personal, occupational, and civic life. It means we want to increase both their sensitivity and their integrity in that struggle.

Finally, we have also suggested that the ordained minister is concerned for and has a role in forming a public ethic. That formation is not to be left either to take care of itself or to be dictated by the media, public education, and government policy, much as all these impinge on it. Cultural leadership in this realm is also a responsibility of church and synagogue.

The chief arena of our own pastoral work is the congregation. A good metaphor for our moral role with the congregation is "coach." The coach knows a lot about the game and is usually a veteran player. The coach teaches, and directs practice. But the coach also knows he or she does not star on the field. The players are the ones who win or lose the game. We are concerned about the quality of communal life inside the church of course. But the moral action we are more concerned about is out there in the world—in the board room, the shop, the city council chambers, the bedroom, the classroom, and over the backyard fence. That is the main playing field. We can only coach parishioners for their work out there and send them to it in hopeful and respectful trust. The pastor is not a moral puppeteer.

European educators have for some years converted a half-word into a useful term for the moral nurture and guidance of adults, *agogy*. The word is familiar, of course, as part of *pedagogy* or *demagogic*. One pair of authors speak of three types of intervention in the inner life of another: psychotherapy, pastoral care, and *agogy*. Agogy means literally to give guidance—as an educator or a parent might. It "aims to . . . exert influence governed by ideals or normativity."[1] But *agogy* also expresses something of the style in exerting that influence. Malcolm Knowles, an American educator, prefers *andragogy*, opposing it to pedagogy, thereby making the point that in coaching adults we are less directive than with children. We engage in mutual inquiry; we evoke self-teaching by the other. We affirm the other's moral worth by exercising such respect. We build moral self-reliance, and we coach for moral action on the playing fields where that person lives out life. In this chapter, then, we look at the agogic occasions in parish life, with special concern for developing moral maturity in the congregation.

Leadership of the entire congregation presents certain analogies to counseling work with individuals. Counseling hopes to strengthen a sense of self, accepting one's personal history, developing clear boundaries between self and the world, and a moral character that guides reflection and action. With the congregation also, we nurture the sense of strong Christian identity as a unit of God's people, with a history rooted in Israel, a people separate enough from the world, while serving it, that we can be its loving moral critic and urge it on toward God's shalom.

---

1. Quoted by Jacob Firet, 1986, p. 103, from C. W. du Boeuff and P. C. Kuiper.

Worship

The most significant occasion in congregational life is the weekly service of worship. The central purpose of worship is *not* moral education, and by discussing moral nurture through worship I risk some distortion. Worship is not a pep rally for moral virtue; it is not a forum for debating pro and con the public moral dilemma of the week.

Worship celebrates the worth-ship of God. It is a human activity, to be sure, but it is directed toward God, in prayer and praise. Theologically understood, its primary actions consist of a "vertical" dialogue between God and the human community. Hymns, prayers, and offering (including bread and wine brought for Eucharist) constitute action oriented toward God; that is balanced in turn by the reading and exposition of scripture and the distribution of communion in movements toward the people from God.

The "horizontal" discussions in worship—congregational business, announcements for the good of the parish, organizing for community action—must take second place, appropriate as they are to a gathering of Christians. In the setting of worship, these parish concerns take on special meanings as activities of the people of God. If they begin to dominate, however, Godward religious consciousness will wither.

Our peoplehood (I Pet. 2:10) is established in the God-relation that is nourished in worship—an event in which the God-relation is proclaimed and acted out. When the event is sidetracked, for whatever reason, or when worship becomes so routine as to lose its sense of holy eventfulness, the community's identity is in jeopardy.

Humanly speaking, what happens to us as we worship is important. In praising God we rehearse—we express and thereby reinforce our understanding of—the milieu of our human existence, which is the governance and grace of God. The governance and grace of the biblical God have moral implications. Therefore, the planner and leader of worship will attend to certain moral dimensions in the service. Lacking them, the worship may be idolatrous, directed toward a god who is not God.

1. First, the worship planner-leader will see to it that the service expresses *concern for the human neighbor*. Prayers include intercessions for the peace of the world, the welfare of the poor and disinherited. Besides the texts from the lectionary, the occasions of the secular and civic calendar may prompt special concerns: on Labor Day Sunday, for the unemployed, for the underpaid, and for the structures of labor, management, and the economic life; at Thanksgiving, for good stewardship of the abundance of the earth; and at the "Festival of the Christian Home" (Mother's Day) for right relations in family life. Prayers from the tradition may be supplemented by prayers from today, and by free prayer. One of the early twentieth-century classics that still offers good models is Walter Rauschenbusch's *Prayers of the Social Awakening*.

2. *Confession* gives voice to our knowledge of moral failure, sharpening our moral sensitivities meanwhile. We fail as stewards; we fail in our sensitivity to the needs of persons close to us; we fail in our fidelity to God. Confession also expresses our enmeshment in the corporate community, the world's oppressive ways, its warfare, its disdain for the weak and handicapped and defeated. We confess sin, beyond our petty and specific sins.

3. The service also sets forth our *commitment*. The offertory moment (best *after* the service of the Word) is much more than a collection of money, whether it includes a presentation of the communion elements or not. These are symbols of our self-offering in service to God by way of service to neighbor. Revivalist churches have an altar call. Others often label the final hymn a "hymn of commitment." Whatever the form, this third element should be a regular experience of the people at worship—the pledge of self-giving, the experience of moral resolve.

4. Preaching, of course, provides occasion for more *explicit moral instruction* and exhortation. We break open the words of a text, so that the Word may address us. And there are moral implications. Without reverting to biblicism, we .

review and reflect on the meanings of the law for us. Attending to the law rehearses the claims that moral structures have on us, and it reminds us of our moral seriousness as believers. The gospel complements the law, promising reconciliation to the penitent.

There are various ways we can prevent preaching from falling into moralistic sermonizing aimed at unheeding people. Such preaching does little for moral insight or action. One strategy is to wrestle with pairs of mutually contradictory texts. The puzzle draws the listener into the dilemmas presented by the variegated scriptural language and tradition. One thinks immediately of a range of contrasting biblical statements: on divorce (Luke 16:18; Matt. 5:31-32 or 19:9); on family allegiance (Exod. 20:12—the fifth commandment on filial loyalty; and Matt. 19:29, or Luke 14:26—on disowning family ties); on giving (e.g., Deut. 14:22—on tithing; and Luke 18:22, "sell all you have," or Mark 12:42-43, on the widow's mite); on respect for the state (Romans 13; Revelation 13); on wealth (e.g., Ps. 112—on the righteous, wealthy person; and Jesus' needle's eye warning, Mark 10:25); on truth-telling, with a story like Rahab's deceit (Joshua 2) and injunctions against falsehoods (Exod. 23:1; or Prov. 21:28). We take this tack not to be clever, but to nurture reflection and a more nuanced understanding of moral complexity.

Occasionally, the same approach may be used in a topical sermon, addressing some public issue of the day. The preacher interprets and even persuades on each side of a controversy, without resolving the tension. If this is done, however, a unifying theological affirmation must be offered, lest the proclamation be lost in the tangle of moral point and counterpoint.

For example, in a sermon on Christian truthfulness, illustrations can range from the necessity for deception in international espionage to the physician's struggle for candor with a vulnerable patient about a probably terminal cancer. It may focus on both political and personal life. It may pit a rule-oriented kind of ethics against a consequentialist, end-justifies-the-means kind. But above it all, the sermon should be announcing the quest for truth as a profound and fundamental response to God. Using John, for instance, it can stress the nonlegalistic but demanding Christian life-way, one that reflects the spirit of the Christ who says, "I am the way and the truth and the life."

Some congregational learning strategies relate to preaching. Ministers schedule "back-talk" sessions after service to expand the chance for the church's growth as a community of moral discourse. Preaching is a one-way kind of talk; but Christian moral reflection needs dialogue. In a sermon for a back-talk Sunday, a pastor may even raise specific points for communal discussion. Back-talk sessions invite the laity to contribute their expertise, from their work-world, civic, and family life experiences. Such sessions show respect for the laity and their moral seriousness. Rightly conducted, they can also enhance the skills of moral reflection.

Inviting discussion in advance of preaching is another way to achieve some of these same goals. A preparation group of church members will meet early in the week to go over the text for the following Sunday. The preacher may introduce the Bible passage or passages, and may address particular questions to the group. Some moral implications of Scripture will usually emerge; they may be deepened if the leader shares his or her own concerns without railroading the discussion. Sermon preparation groups cannot write a preacher's sermon, but they can assist in important ways—by disclosing the level of maturity that is to be addressed by the speaker, by providing illustrations, by broadening and deepening hermeneutical insight, and by training one more group of people as critical listeners and better theologians of the pew.

Teaching and Learning

The range of content in the church's teaching life is wide. Adult education committees sponsor Bible study groups, courses on church history and Christian belief, and church-and-culture series on music, play-readings, or films.

Alongside these, a perennial theme is Christian morals in relation to contemporary values and contemporary society. Three caveats and some suggestions are in order, to help the coach at this point.

Problems. I label one nonproductive trap in moral education the "ain't it awful" syndrome. People spend their time bemoaning the low state of public and private morality in what is little more than dignified gossip. The danger, of course, is that the group takes pride in its own virtue, like the Pharisee, praying at the temple. The group members may somehow think they have achieved moral growth by discussing the shortcomings of other people. "Ain't it awful" sessions do have some virtue in reinforcing a group's own standards by the way of negation, but it would be far better directly to address the standard-setting tasks of Christian love. And far better yet is a search for ways to reach out to these who have been so glibly dismissed as immoral. It is better to struggle with the question, What can we compassionately do about it? than to bask in self-righteous complacency.

Another danger, in more sophisticated moral reflection, is a resigned relativism. At its worst, this can amount to little more than a dogmatic assertion that all values and truth-claims are relative. (All, that is, except this one assertion, which is absolutely true!) Once one admits there are exceptions to every rule, that there are wide differences in the mores among different cultures, that there are at least two sides to nearly every question, and that even moral standards in a culture seem to evolve and change, a person wonders where to find any solid ground. (A favorite *New Yorker* cartoon of mine shows two tormented men in hell. One says to the other, "The hell of it is, the things I'm in here for aren't sins any more.")

Moreover, once it is clear that Christians do not perform the right and the good so as to gain heaven for themselves—thus mocking, by this self-seeking, the whole idea of altruism—people feel more lost at sea. This is the trap of self-justifying legalism. If God is a forgiving God who gives full acceptance to eleventh-hour workers

(Matt. 20:1-16) and the death-bed penitent, legalists say to themselves, "Why struggle now?" They ask, "What do morals matter?"

With a patient, theologically sensitive ear, the good moral counselor must be prepared to help a group grow beyond Phariseeism, beyond defeatist relativism, and beyond naive religious legalism.

Method. Because our goals are moral growth rather than the production of ethical analyses for an elite leadership, we will attend to both content and group process as we plan adult moral education. Lives change more amidst the mutual support of small groups where commitment is nurtured than they do in larger, passive audiences. Retreats are ideal for this coaching, because they provide the sustained time where the kinds of problems just mentioned can surface and be worked through. They also offer the kind of intimate atmosphere in which commitments can develop. Retreats can build around a theme of interest to a particular segment of a congregation: the Christian in business; sexual ethics today; pacifism and just wars in a nuclear age; parenting and teenage values. The National Conference of Catholic Bishops, and parallel bodies in other major denominations, have recently prepared excellent study documents on both the ethics of nuclear armament and the American economy. These booklets are valuable resources for either an extended retreat or a weekly study series.

A retreat offers time for recreation, table fellowship, private and corporate worship, and study. It should be planned with a variety of vehicles for learning—films, roleplaying, debates, various sorts of Bible study. One of the best vehicles for growth in moral insight is the open-ended case study. Such a case study is always based on a real-life dilemma, so the complexities of ordinary living enter in. Stereotyping, strawman villains, and simplistic answers are avoided. The narrative is written so as to involve any alert reader from the start. Often it is short enough to be read during the first five minutes of a session without advance preparation. Paperback case books on various areas of concern are more and more available from the Association for Case Teaching—family life, church and society dilemmas, business ethics, global development, and American policy. An annotated bibliography of hundreds of individual cases is also available.[2] Teaching notes accompany most cases ordered from the bibliography.

My emphasis on retreats does not mean the weekly or fortnightly adult study group is passé. Far from it. We need more such groups. Here also, the case study format is helpful; most cases are provocative enough that the homework will get done.

One of the best settings for moral growth comes about when a group of people with similar occupations meets regularly for long enough to trust group members to use their own stories as cases. Managers ask for help about the morality of a plant closing, about firing a man in his late 50s, about handling employee alcoholism, about bribes and "consultant" fees overseas. Parents discuss with one another their standards for homework time, the use of the family car, keeping hours, curtailing the use of alcohol and dope in the schools, parental teaching on contraception. Social workers and teachers shore up one another against burnout, consult on public intervention in cases of child or spouse abuse, develop new ideas for professional and public policy. In Germany, in the decades after World War II, there were large-scale church-initiated meetings by professional groups, the "Evangelical Academies." Their agenda was policy development and mutual support in professional and moral concerns. Both Christians and non-Christians participated.

Service and action groups often provide unusually high motivation for learning. A group intent on prison reform will be forced to do homework on the nature of the corrections system, and the ethics of justice and mercy. A group taking up soup kitchen service can easily move to deeper understandings of welfare policy. Action without

2. Box 243, Simsbury, CT 06070, or c/o Librarian, 409 Prospect Street, New Haven, CT 06510

reflection can be misguided. Study without at least some playout in the community's life can become sterile and self-satisfied enough to represent a spiritual hazard rather than an effort at faithfulness.

Controversy

Rightly exploited, the life of the congregation itself is as important a resource for coaching in moral life as the formal class or ad hoc discussion group. The congregation's degree of interpersonal honesty and compassion, its sense of stewardship and social outreach, and its pattern of decision making all combine to promote or impoverish the moral experience of those whose spiritual nourishment the church provides. So too do the ways the congregation handles conflict, large or small.

Controversy is prominent in the learning menu of congregational life. Four rules of thumb about controversy in the church will help the moral counselor. First, use the energy generated by controversy. Contention means emotional involvement, and involvement is better than apathy. Controversy can be destructive, without doubt, but emotion means people care.

Second, look beneath the surface. If an issue seems petty, we need to look more than skin deep to see what nerve is being touched. A dispute over repainting the sanctuary may be a power struggle between two committees. Or it may subtly reflect deep-seated differences about the church's style of worship or about antiquated or updated relations to modern culture. It may reflect a plurality of social class that the church could acknowledge and celebrate. Reaction to a change of pronoun in a Scripture lesson may come from genuine concern for clear grammar or from profound puzzlement and prejudice over feminism and our always evolving language about God.

Third, use controversy for training in the arts of reconciliation. The art is necessary for lay ministry in the weekday world. Everyone meets controversy—in marriage and the family, among friends, at work, in neighborhood and civic life. Whether it leads to enmity or forgiveness depends on the way the parties to the disputes respond. The church can think of itself as a miniature peace academy, training its participants in conflict resolution.

In church, I first learned how to overcome my fear of argument, and my ability to speak up to someone who seemed overpowering and intimidating. I learned to say, "My friend, I think we disagree about that," instead of quietly harboring resentment and proceeding less honestly with the friendship. That learning has served me well outside the church.

In church we can learn to objectify an issue—to talk about the facts and positions in a case rather than the personalities. Extrapolated to the global scale, learning of that sort can prevent the fear-mongering and demagoguery that usually precede the decay of diplomacy into war.

Fourth, exploit controversy for moral growth. It offers fertile ground. Seeing the tent city referred to in the previous chapter, many people felt the camp-out tarnished the city's reputation and violated proper decorum. Others, however, including some members of the city's business and political leadership, were prompted to look into the needs for temporary shelter and new housing. Discussions between those two points of view precipitated moral growth—and action. The moral counselor can capitalize on such community debates, raising them for discussion in the midst of congregational life, and thus taking one more step toward improving the church as a community of moral discourse and service.

Like the grain of sand troubling an oyster but making for a pearl, a small controversy may lead to study and wider vision. Given good leadership, a potentially controversial step taken by one unit within a church can lead to a new church-wide sense of mission: a Sunday school penpal project with children in Nicaragua; a benevolence committee's assistance to the World Council of Churches' project on racism; a college student group's campus picketing over apartheid and divestment. As coach for the congregation's moral maturity, the pastor will not back away from controversy. Rather, he or she will expect it as one of the growing pains of parish life, and one of the potential resources in the task of moral counsel.

Nevertheless, the Commandments?

Our moral counselor metaphor has led us to stress a person's intrinsic moral integrity—a person's autonomy—rather than mere obedience to extrinsic behavioral codes. One might charge that this position arises from necessity. In American culture, the authority of the church and its ordained ministry is moral rather than juridical. That is, its power is exercised through persuasion rather than in enforceable injunction and law. In a voluntaristic church, and in a political arrangement that separates church and state, this charge would have it that we have to go this route, that we have no other choice.

For us, however, this arrangement is itself a moral choice based on justice, respect, and a knowledge of the dangers in both political and religious autocracy.

Since the days of Ernst Troeltsch, an oversimplified but useful typology has served to help describe church traditions. It ranges church groups along a spectrum from the broad and highly tolerant "church" to the narrow and highly disciplined "sect," withdrawn from society. There is little question but that today some movement by the loosely organized mainline churches away from their acculturation and in the direction of the "sect"-type end of this scale is in order. We need a more disciplined community. Should it come about, however, even that movement will mostly be a collective change arising within the community, not something engineered by clergy decree. Learned priests and pastors once taught a relatively unlearned people the rules of God and claimed to govern their moral life. In a highly literate society the clergy take a different role. They must work with people, rather than above them. Furthermore, a protected moral enclave is morally suspect if it is fleeing from the world instead of responsible toward it. The world needs moral leadership from the church, not the church's withdrawal.

But how can moral leadership be exercised in such a pluralistic church and in so secular a society as ours? For many people, the question begs for moral absolutes, and hard-nosed systems of enforcement. These folk will be disappointed with a book that says the morally concerned pastor does not deal mainly with behavioral norms. Where is the clear voice that some things are right and some things are wrong? The questions always arise when we invite moral growth more urgently than behavioral obedience.

Put the matter in terms of a three-stage growth. In spite of our indispensable deference to it, the theologian cannot ultimately be satisfied with the usual secular meanings of autonomy. At first—as children and as babes in faith—we allow others to shape our life with behavioral rules. Call that stage *heteronomy*. We move on from that to *autonomy*, a necessary developmental stage when we gain strength to take our own action in the world. Beyond that, and coming more and more into our deepest awareness, is the sense that our moral lives are finally grounded in the God-relation. We are not so much "autonomous" as free in God. "I worked harder than any of them," said Paul, comparing himself to other apostles, "though it was not I, but the grace of God which is with me" (I Cor. 15:10). "Make me a captive, Lord, and then I shall be free," says the hymn. It is life in covenant.

We may dare to call this third stage *theonomy* so long as the Creator-creature line is clearly enough maintained that we never claim to have the Ultimate within our own sweaty grasp. Blurring the line like that, we usually proceed (self-righteously, whether conscious of it or not) to damn all contrary opinion, even if it is morally serious. And that step is not a moral victory but a defeat.

In nurturing people toward theonomy we will often preach and teach the law of God. We will argue for behavior of this sort and that sort. But we will give reasons—from Bible and tradition, from contemporary Christian thought, and from our own religious experience—inviting others to hear in our words the Word of God. Yes, we *will* be saying that some things are right and some things are wrong. But the injunctions will spring from thoughtful faith and a moral respect for the human neighbor rather than fear of the different neighbor, or pride and its imperious or manipulative relation to that neighbor.

T.V. talkshow host Ted Koppel said one night, "Moses didn't come down the mountain with ten *suggestions*." As moral counselor, the minister represents—as does the church—far more than a few suggestions for living in the daily round. Week upon week, we point to fundamental moral and spiritual reality. Philosophers have called God the Absolute. We are to give God our whole allegiance—heart, mind, soul, strength; we are to acknowledge God's claim on us. We do so by means of thinking that assumes God's being—by theology, and by means of worship, and by reflective moral action. All are built around the torah of God, and around the way, the life, and the truth in Christ.

We cannot speak for God in human language, however, without at the same time acknowledging our human limits of mind and heart. Therefore, we do not codify all God's laws into brittle, behavioral rules. For us Christians, the moral life is deeper than behavior because we ourselves are heirs of God's mercy. So we dare not pretend that any transgressors are beyond the reach of God's love. We proclaim law *and* gospel. In utter seriousness, but with a light heart, we coach and nurture both compassion and moral integrity in the midst of our communities of faith. The issue, ultimately, is in the hands of God.

Bibliography

Books

Alperovitz, Gar, and Jeff Faux. *Rebuilding America*. New York: Pantheon Books, 1984.

American Hospital Association. *Values in Conflict: Resolving Ethical Issues in Hospital Care*. Chicago: American Hospital Association, 1985.

Andrews, Lewis M. *To Thine Own Self Be True: The Re-Birth of Values in the New Ethical Therapy*. Garden City, N.Y.: Doubleday, 1987.

Armstrong, Richard Stoll. *The Pastor as Evangelist*. Philadelphia: Westminster Press, 1984.

Bainton, Roland. *What Christianity Says About Sex, Love and Marriage*. New York: Association Press, 1957.

Barr, James. *The Bible in the Modern World*. New York: Harper & Row, Publishers, 1973.

Beauchamp, Tom L., and James F. Childress. *Principles of Biomedical Ethics* (2nd ed.). New York: Oxford University Press, 1983.

Becker, Russell. *Family Pastoral Care*. Englewood Cliffs, N.J.: Prentice-Hall, 1965.

Bellah, Robert Neelly, et al. *Habits of the Heart: Individualism and Commitment in American Life*. Berkeley: University of California Press, 1985.

Birch, Bruce C., and Larry L. Rasmussen. *Bible and Ethics in the Christian Life*. Minneapolis: Augsburg Publishing House, 1976.

Bok, Sisela. *Lying*. New York: Random House, 1978.

172 ~ THE MINISTER AS MORAL COUNSELOR

Bonhoeffer, Dietrich. *The Cost of Discipleship.* New York: Macmillan, 1963.
Browning, Don. *The Moral Context of Pastoral Care.* Philadelphia: Westminster Press, 1976.
Brueggemann, Walter. *The Prophetic Imagination.* Philadelphia: Fortress Press, 1978.
Brunner, Heinrich Emil. *Dogmatics.* Philadelphia: Westminster Press, 1950.

Clapp, Steve. *Teenage Sexuality: Local Church and Christian Home Program Guide.* Champaign, Ill.: C-4 Publications, 1985.
Clebsch, William A., and Charles R. Jaekle. *Pastoral Care in Historical Perspective.* New York: Jason Aronson, 1964.
Coles, Robert. *The Moral Life of Children.* Boston: Atlantic Monthly Press, 1986.

Dykstra, Craig, and Sharon Parks, eds. *Faith Development and Fowler.* Birmingham, Ala.: Religious Education Press, 1986.

Erikson, Erik H., ed. *The Challenge of Youth.* Garden City, N.Y.: Doubleday, 1965.
Erikson, Erik H. *Identity and the Life Cycle.* New York: International Universities Press, 1959.

Farley, Margaret A. *Personal Commitments.* San Francisco: Harper & Row, Publishers, 1986.
Festinger, Leon. *A Theory of Cognitive Dissonance.* Stanford: Stanford University Press, 1957.
Firet, Jacob. *Dynamics in Pastoring.* Grand Rapids, Mich.: Wm. B. Eerdmans Publishing Co., 1986.
Fortune, Marie. *Sexual Violence: The Unmentionable Sin.* New York: Pilgrim Press, 1983.
Fowler, James W. *Stages of Faith.* San Francisco: Harper & Row, Publishers, 1981.
Frank, Jerome. *Persuasion and Healing.* New York: Schocken Books, 1963.
Frankl, Viktor. *Man's Search for Meaning: An Introduction to Logotherapy.* Boston: Beacon Press, 1963.
Freeman, Forster. *Readiness for Ministry Through Spiritual Direction.* Washington, D.C.: Alban Institute, 1986.

Geertz, Clifford. *The Interpretation of Cultures.* New York: Basic Books, 1973.
Gilligan, Carol. *In a Different Voice.* Cambridge, Mass.: Harvard University Press, 1982.
Goethals, Gregor. *The TV Ritual: Worship at the Video Altar.* Boston: Beacon Press, 1981.

Gurin, G. J. Veroff, and S. Field. *Americans View Their Mental Health.* New York: Basic Books, 1960.

Gustafson, James M. *Treasure in Earthen Vessels: The Church as a Human Community.* New York: Harper & Brothers, 1961.

Gustafson, James, et al. *Moral Education: Five Lectures.* Cambridge, Mass.: Harvard University Press, 1970.

Halberstam, David. *The Best and the Brightest.* New York: Random House, 1972.

Hiltner, Seward. *Preface to Pastoral Theology.* Nashville/New York: Abingdon Press, 1958.

Holmes, Urban T., III. *The Future Shape of Ministry: A Theological Projection.* New York: Seabury Press, 1971.

Houck, John W., and Oliver F. Williams. *Full Value: Cases in Christian Business Ethics.* New York: Harper & Row, Publishers, 1981.

Kelsey, David. *The Uses of Scripture in Recent Theology.* Philadelphia: Fortress Press, 1975.

Kohlberg, Lawrence. *The Philosophy of Moral Development: Moral Stages and the Idea of Justice.* (Essays on Moral Development, vol. 1). San Francisco, Harper & Row, Publishers, 1981.

Lasch, Christopher. *The Culture of Narcissism.* New York: W. W. Norton & Co., 1972.

Leech, Kenneth. *Spiritual Friend: The Practice of Christian Spirituality.* San Francisco: Harper & Row, Publishers, 1977.

Lochhead, D. *The Liberation of the Bible.* Toronto: Student Christian Movement of Canada, 1977.

McNeill, John. *A History of the Cure of Souls.* New York: Harper & Brothers, 1951.

Maslow, A. H. *Motivation and Personality.* New York: Harper & Brothers, 1954.

Massialis, Byron G., and Jack Zevin. *Creative Encounters in the Classroom.* New York: John Wiley & Sons, 1967.

Meilaender, Gilbert C. *The Theory and Practice of Virtue.* Notre Dame: University of Notre Dame Press, 1984.

Menninger, Karl. *Whatever Became of Sin?* New York: Hawthorn Books, 1973.

Minear, Paul. *Images of the Church in the New Testament.* Philadelphia: Westminster Press, 1960.

———. *To Die and To Live: Christ's Resurrection and Christian Vocation.* New York: Seabury Press, 1977.

National Council of Catholic Bishops. *Economic Justice for All: Pastoral Letter on Catholic Social Teaching and the U.S. Economy.* Washington, D.C.: U.S. Catholic Conference, 1986.

Nelson, James B., and Joanne Smith Rohricht. *Human Medicine: Ethical Perspectives on Today's Medical Issues.* Minneapolis: Augsburg Publishing House, 1984.

Neuhaus, Richard John. *The Naked Public Square: Religion and Democracy in America.* Grand Rapids, Mich.: Wm. B. Eerdmans Publishing Co., 1984.

Niebuhr, H. Richard. *The Responsible Self: An Essay in Christian Moral Philosophy.* New York: Harper & Row, Publishers, 1963.

————. *The Purpose of the Church and Its Ministry.* New York: Harper & Brothers, 1956.

Niebuhr, Reinhold. *An Interpretation of Christian Ethics.* New York: Harper & Brothers, 1935.

Oden, Thomas C. *After Therapy What?* Springfield, Ill.: Charles C. Thomas, Publisher, 1974.

Oglesby, William B., Jr. *Biblical Themes for Pastoral Care.* Nashville: Abingdon, 1980.

Outka, Gene. *Agape: An Ethical Analysis.* New Haven, Conn: Yale University Press, 1972.

Piaget, Jean. *The Moral Judgment of the Child.* New York: Free Press, 1965.

Pruyser, Paul. *The Minister as Diagnostician.* Philadelphia: Westminster Press, 1976.

Raths, Louis E., Merrill Harmin, and Sidney Simon. *Values and Teaching.* Columbus, Ohio: C. E. Merrill Books, 1966.

Rauschenbusch, Walter. *Prayers of the Social Awakening.* Boston: Pilgrim Press, 1910.

Rieff, Philip. *The Triumph of the Therapeutic: Uses of Faith After Freud.* New York: Harper & Row, Publishers, 1966.

Roberts, William O., Jr. *Initiation to Adulthood.* New York: Pilgrim Press, 1982.

Rossman, Parker, and Gaylord Noyce. *Helping People Care on the Job.* Valley Forge, Pa.: Judson Books, 1985.

Schön, Donald A. *The Reflective Practitioner: How Professionals Think in Action.* New York: Basic Books, 1983.

Shelp, Earl E., and Ronald H. Sunderland. *The Pastor as Prophet.* New York: Pilgrim Press, 1985.

Siegel, Bernard S. *Love, Medicine and Miracles.* New York: Harper & Row, Publishers, 1986.

Strole, L. *Mental Health in the Metropolis: The Midtown Manhattan Study.* New York: McGraw-Hill, 1962.

Szasz, Thomas S. *The Myth of Mental Illness: Foundations of a Theory of Personal Conduct.* New York: Harper & Row, Publishers (Hoeber Medical Division), 1961.

Thornton, Edward. *Theology and Pastoral Counseling.* Englewood Cliffs, N.J.: Prentice-Hall, 1964.

Thurneysen, Eduard. *A Theology of Pastoral Care.* Richmond, Va.: John Knox Press, 1962.

Tillich, Paul. *The Courage to Be.* New Haven, Conn.: Yale University Press, 1952.

Underwood, Ralph L. *Empathy and Confrontation in Pastoral Care.* Philadelphia: Fortress Press, 1985.

Whitehead, Alfred North. *Religion in the Making.* Cambridge: Cambridge University Press, 1926.

Wicks, Robert J., Richard D. Parsons, and Donald E. Capps, eds. *Clinical Handbook of Pastoral Counseling.* New York: Paulist Press, 1985.

Winter, Gibson. *The New Creation as Metropolis.* New York: Macmillan, 1963.

Yoder, John Howard. *The Politics of Jesus.* Grand Rapids: Wm. B. Eerdmans Publishing Co., 1972.

Articles

Gustafson, James M. "The Minister as Moral Counselor." *Proceedings,* 1982. Association for Professional Education for Ministry.

——. "Political Images of the Ministry," in Underwood, Kenneth, ed., *The Church, The University, and Social Policy: The Danforth Study of Campus Ministries.* Middletown, Conn.: Wesleyan University Press, 1969, pp. 247-62.

Kohlberg, Lawrence. "Stages of Moral Development as a Basis for Moral Education," in Munsey, Brenda, ed. *Moral Development, Moral Education, and Kohlberg.* Birmingham, Ala.: Religious Education Press, 1980, pp. 15-98.

Mollica, Richard F., Frederick J. Streets, Joseph Boscarino, and Fritz C. Redlich, "A Community Study of Formal Pastoral Counseling Activities of the Clergy." *American Journal of Psychiatry* 143 (March 1986): 323-28.

Noyce, Gaylord B. "How Shall We Use the Bible Now?" *The Christian Century* 96 (April 4, 1979): 370-73.

————. "The Dilemmas of Christians in Business." *The Christian Century* 98 (August 12, 1981): 802-4.

Royce, James E., S. J. "Alcohol and Other Drug Dependencies," in Wicks, Robert J., Richard D. Parsons, and Donald E. Capps, eds. *Clinical Handbook of Pastoral Counseling.* New York: Paulist Press, 1985, pp. 502-19.